1/31/2013
Dear Barbara,
Your flowers for
David were so special, the
loving touches said so much.
Now, relax and enjoy
sharing my Dad's story.
Love, Joanie

It Was My Pleasure

Biography of Arthur T Doyle

By Joan Doyle

In grateful and loving memory of

my father and mother,

Art and Fran

68th wedding anniversary

Acknowledgements

I am most grateful to...

- my Dad for sharing his life story.
- my siblings: Arthur, Barbie, Nancy, Mary, Carol, Claire and Debbie who helped enormously from start to finish. They encouraged, supported, critiqued, suggested, advised, loved and so much more.
- my friends, community members and colleagues who each contributed according to his or her gifts and talents.
- Jerry Reilly who took the final phase of this book in hand, generously and ably helping me to navigate the sometimes murky waters of self- publication.

Table of Contents

Preface

The first inkling that I might write this came in 2003, as I listened to Dad during his 90th birthday party. He and Mom, who had suffered a serious stroke the previous October, were there encircled by their family, friends and neighbors. Memories blended with the afternoon sunlight filling the room, drawing us into its warm embrace. Dad regaled us with anecdotes from years gone by; while Mom, who was in great form that day, offered some priceless comments of her own. It was a day made to be remembered.

Six months later on a bitterly cold January evening Mom went home to God. Dad lost the love of his life, his daily companion, his other half. In the months following her death, at some profound level, we began to realize that we had lost not only our Mother, but also any further chance to discover more about her life, to have answers to questions we had not thought to ask, but that rose up within our minds and hearts now that she was gone.

Later on a long, lazy fall afternoon when the leaves were at the height of their colorful glory, Dad and I were relaxing in the living room of Barbie and Dick's home in Plymouth when I casually asked, "Dad, tell me something about the different places where you have lived". Unexpectedly, my question opened an inner door. What flowed out in bits and pieces over many afternoons together, is the story you are about to read.

Sometimes I asked questions. More common were the days when I sat back quietly letting him reminisce at will. Those times often brought forth deeper sharing, revealing more of who Dad was, how he tried to live his life, how he approached death. These seemed precious memories for us who still grieve our loss. They may also create a connective bridge for the younger generations, who have not known him in his prime or perhaps have not known him at all.

Dad agreed to the writing of this biography. He seemed to like the idea, since he said to me from time to time, “Did I tell you about this yet?" As I listened, another story, one more memory unfolded.

Thus, it is his story, his remembrances, woven together with strands of history, plus a tad of artistic license.

Irish Catholic Bostonian

The afternoon was turning hot as Dr. Johnson walked purposefully past the rectory, turned up Pontiac Street, and began the steep climb. Once he passed the stone ledge area the street began to level out. He paused a moment to catch his breath, admiring the stately wooden triple- deckers that faced him in all directions. No one was out on the broad back porches at this early hour, but probably would be as the summer evening cooled down. Soon he reached Hillside Street, easily locating number 72, where he had delivered a baby boy just two years before. He hoped this birth would go as well.

James Doyle met him at the door. A quiet Irish immigrant who served on a U.S. battleship during the Spanish-American War, James was a member of Boston's Police Force and proud to be so. He said nothing beyond the basic greeting, at once ushering Dr. Johnson into the large airy bedroom off the kitchen where Catherine was anxiously awaiting his arrival. She was a proud Irish woman from the tiny country town of Tubbercurry, who had a sturdy frame, piercing blue eyes and fine brown hair pinned up in a bun. She had left Ireland a few years earlier in her late twenties. Catherine and James, both natives of County Sligo in the west of Ireland, met in the Roxbury area of Boston, courted and were married in April of 1910.

Everything was in readiness for the delivery. Mrs. Drury, an affable woman from the neighborhood had come over to help out as needed. The bureau drawer, which would be the baby's first cradle, was fully lined with soft fresh smelling blankets, waiting for the little one to snuggle in. A healthy howl announced the arrival of their second son, Arthur Thomas. It was August 11, 1913. Life seemed good for them as they gently gathered the newborn into their arms, their hearts and their home.

Arthur's older brother was named James (Jimmy). Soon after Art's second birthday a baby girl, Helen joined this close knit family. In the following years George (1917), Anne (1921) and finally a set of twins, Paul and Frank arrived (1923) completing the circle.

The first years of Arthur's life were full of wondrous new experiences. As a youngster he was intrigued, peering through the living room window, watching the herd of cows meandering down from Bradley's farm at the top of the hill. On a fair day, if his mother was otherwise occupied, he might sneak out of the house to follow them straight down the street. Not being allowed to cross over at Brigham Circle, he would simply stand aside and watch them head out to the grazing fields in Brookline, knowing that they would certainly return again in the late afternoon.

He felt important once he was old enough to put the cardboard sign in the front window telling Mike Walsh, the iceman, how much ice was needed for the day. The sign was four cornered and depending how you turned it, it allowed for orders from twenty-five cents to one dollar. Relatively soon after the sign was visible, a horse- drawn wagon would come trotting down the street, pulling up outside the house. Mike hoisted the big cold chunk of ice onto a dark skinned leather protector draped across his shoulder and walked into the kitchen. There he skillfully placed the slab of ice in its proper spot atop the wooden icebox. The food on the shelves below was safe for another while.

With no televisions or computers yet, it was a real treat to attend a movie at the local picture house, usually on a Saturday afternoon. Since the films were silent, the piano player was a vital part of the whole experience. Cheers went up, sometimes even a standing ovation, as the pianist strode down the aisle, took his place at the piano, uncovered the keyboard and began filling the theater with the exact strains of music that brought the scenes of the film to life.

Art was less than thrilled in his youth by the oft repeated process for doing the seemingly endless piles of family wash. He watched as the soap stone sink in the kitchen filled with piping hot soapy water, sending clouds of steam out into the whole room. Soon the ripple- surfaced scrub board came into play, that, plus loads of energy were required to clean out the dirt. Next the clothes had to be thoroughly rinsed. Finally, came the tough process of wringing out as much water as possible so the clothes were ready to be hung up to dry. On a clear day he trailed behind his Mother onto the back porch to help supply her with the clothespins for hanging line after line of wet clothes. If it were a damp wintry day, the mound of wet clothes had to be draped across lines throughout the house or carefully strewn near the stove to dry. For his mother, this was a necessary part of her housework, for Art, this was a mess.

When the day finally came for his formal schooling to begin, Art's mother smoothed back his blond wavy hair, took his hand in hers, and walked him down the steep hill, across the trolley car tracks on Huntington Avenue and into the noisy school yard of the Farragut School. Since Art was a friendly kid he soon forgot the strangeness of his surroundings, latched onto a group of kids kicking a ball around and from then on he simply joined in whatever was afoot. Kindergarten passed from one season to the next, finishing all too quickly. He needed to say good-bye to classmates going on to the local public schools. Others registered, as he did, at Our Lady of Perpetual Help School, known by everyone simply as Mission School.

Mission was a large, red brick, two-building parish school run by the School Sisters of Notre Dame. It had entrances on both Smith Street and St. Alphonsus which placed it literally in the shadow of the Mission Church. Because his brother Jimmy was a third grader, the two of them were able to trudge off to school together each morning. At Mission the boys' and girls' classes were located on different sides of the building. Recess was also in separate parts of the outdoor yard. Sometimes, the boys got to leave the school yard, go down the street a bit to the baseball field on the other side of St. Alphonsus Hall. The school had four classes of each level averaging about 60 students per room. Most students were sons and daughters of immigrant parents, mostly Irish, many of whom had never been able to stay in school beyond the sixth grade.

During these years Art poured his extra-curricular energies into sports of all kinds. He also became an altar boy, mostly serving the early Masses. He felt lucky, now and again, when he got to leave a class to serve a funeral mass.

While still relatively young, he began earning a few extra pennies delivering orders for the local grocery store or selling newspapers after school. His regular paper route took him to Commonwealth Ave. where more than a few of the upscale homes had Irish colleens working in the kitchens. Many a chilly day, one of them invited him in to warm his hands near the large kitchen hearth. Often they offered him hot chocolate and fresh baked cookies before he headed back out to complete his route. Art sold papers outside both of Boston's baseball stadiums: Fenway Park and Braves Field. He devoured the sports news every day, knowing all the stats of his favorite players and team, the Boston Red Sox. When he was six years old they won the World Series, cementing his loyalty to them for life. He would wait eighty-six complete baseball seasons before he would relish that taste of victory again. The 'curse of the Bambino' as it was called, stuck to the Red Sox for decades.

Once in a while if Art still had some papers left, he ventured across the Charles River into Cambridge. The day that Rudolf Valentino died was one of those occasions. He strode up and down the streets around Harvard Square yelling out the news of Valentino's death. People wanted every last detail of the story, so in no time at all the papers were gone. Art raced home, coins jingling in his pockets, delighted with the extra time to play ball at the park.

By 1919, Art's Dad had been on the Boston police force for many years, was highly respected and was in line for a promotion. James had worked hard, taken the civil service exam and was pleased the day he learned that he had come in among the top men and would be in the next group promoted to the rank of sergeant. Catherine was thrilled when he told her the news. Besides being an honor, it also meant an increase in pay which would surely help with their growing family.

But that year there was an unprecedented event in the city. The Boston policemen put forth a strong proposal for improvement of their current wages and working conditions. When negotiators for both sides were unable to reach an agreement, a strike was called. All members of the rank and file, with no exceptions, were expected to join the strike once the final decision came down. Since the public appointment and installation of the new sergeants was not official yet, James had no choice but to join his fellow policemen on the picket lines.

Calvin Coolidge, a native of New Hampshire by birth, but then the Governor of Massachusetts, acted quickly and firmly once apprised of this situation. There was absolutely no precedent for this kind of behavior, policemen on strike. It was not to be tolerated. He considered the strike by the Boston police force a blow against the safety and well-being of the people of the Commonwealth of Massachusetts. The governor would not, he could not, allow this kind of action. Coolidge promptly terminated the employment of each and every man who had participated in the strike. They were immediately fired by executive order of the Governor.

How different it might have been if the strike had begun just a month later, but it did not. Now Art's Dad, with four young children, joined the ranks of the unemployed with almost no financial reserves to fall back upon. Not only that, but he bore the stigma of being unemployed by the public declaration of the governor of the state. Who was going to hire him?

Finding a new job was not an easy task since James, although naturally bright, had scant years of education in Ireland and few marketable skills. He searched for work, following every lead he got. During the months after he lost his job, the darkening circles below his eyes, and the slight downward slope to his shoulders signaled how heavily he carried this weight. He studied hard, taking every civil service exam around. Eventually he was appointed as a school custodian for the city of Boston, being assigned a position in a local high school on Warren Street. Naturally, it paid less, but it was a decent job that would feed and clothe the family.

When Art was old enough, he began to go to his Dad's school right after his own classes ended. With the energy of youth he easily polished off the sweeping, dusting and blackboard cleaning of four to six classrooms in two hours or less. For years Art continued to give his Dad a hand in the late afternoons whenever his schedule allowed.

When it came time for high school, everyone took for granted that Art would go to Mission High, a newly constructed school for which the Doyles, like most parish families, had sacrificed to donate a few of the bricks. The Xaverian Brothers taught the boys while the SSNDs, the same group as at the elementary school, staffed the girls' section. Mission High School was built on Alleghany Street closer to Hillside Street. As luck would have it, the Doyles had by then moved from Hillside to 20 Francis Street which translated into a healthy hike every morning to get to school on time.

During his freshman year at Mission, Art, who had great academic records thus far, was placed in the college courses which included Latin and would include another foreign language in the sophomore year. With the reality of the economic situation of his family and the nation, Art knew college was a dream, not a viable option. In addition, he was failing miserably in Latin. He had absolutely no interest in mastering this subject, while its worth eluded him totally. In fact he wanted out as soon as possible. He spoke with his teachers about changing his direction, especially eliminating the language requirements. The Brothers felt this bright young man ought to continue as he was scheduled so they declined his request, noting that thing might just turn around by the time of his graduation. With the Brothers' decision not to change the college courses on the one hand and his parents' reluctantly granted permission to attend another school on the other, Arthur packed up his books and left Mission High at the end of his first year.

He enrolled at Roxbury Memorial High School located in the Dudley section of town, quite a distance from Francis Street. To arrive by the first class bell was quite an undertaking. It meant being up early, catching a trolley car or bus at Brigham Circle, riding into Dudley Station and walking the rest of the way, sun, rain or snow. Attending this high school proved to be a whole other experience for a young teenager from the Irish Catholic, dominantly white neighborhood around Mission. Daily, Art mixed with students from other ethnic groups, faiths, and differing family backgrounds. He knew no one when he entered there as a sophomore, but he chose this so he would make it work.

Roxbury Memorial, at the time that Art attended, was not strong on discipline. Most teachers were less personally involved in the lives and learnings of the students before them than he had experienced before at Mission. He was going to have to make his own way, which he honestly was well able to do if he put his mind to it. But, Art breezed his way through the next three years. He was bright, quick to catch on, had a good educational background and mastered the required class material with ease. There were no college courses to challenge him, nor did he really push himself to stretch beyond what he needed to study in order to get good grades. No one else urged him along or counseled him about his future. He even took typing one year as an elective which was unusual for a boy at that time. By 1931, just two years after the Crash, he completed his course work and graduated from high school.

Now What?

Times were tough all across the country, Boston was no exception. Horrendous stories of destitution and despair dominated the daily news. People from all walks of life, full of utter desperation, did things like renting a room at a downtown hotel and then jumping to their death on the street below. Dire poverty, mass unemployment, and struggles on many human levels were the common lot. Such was not a hope- filled picture for this lanky young man, venturing into the adult work world for the first time. Taking in the stark reality that surrounded him every day, he pondered his future. He wanted employment like everyone else-yes, but with the enthusiasm of youth he allowed himself to envision good employment with chances for advancement. While Art longed for that ideal job scenario, most people thought themselves totally fortunate to have any means of regular income no matter how small.

If the truth be known, there was another factor driving Art's employment search. His eye and even more so his heart had recently been captured by a petite, vivacious young woman named Frances "Frannie" Keane, who lived a few doors away from him at 12 Francis Street. There were other girls around the neighborhood. Some who would go out of their way to "sort of" run into him on the street or approach him shyly when it was ladies' choice at a local dance, but to no avail. He was smitten.

While finishing his last years in high school, Art worked part-time as a counter clerk in the First National Grocery Store on Huntington Avenue, just around the corner from Francis Street. Fran came in at least once a week to do the shopping. She enjoyed his sense of humor, the gorgeous head of thick wavy hair and the ready smile that filled his face whenever she passed by. During his time there, Art was put in charge of different departments; fruits, vegetables, later salesman at the meat counter, an area for some reason, usually assigned to an Italian. The week-end he took over the meat section someone hung the sign “Doyleano” above the counter.

The best thing about this particular job was definitely not the salary. No, without a doubt, the good part was that it guaranteed that Fran would be coming in to buy weekly groceries. Internally he would shout “right on!” if she forgot something, and had to make an extra trip. She was cute, alert, had a quick wit and eyes that lit up when his humor caught her. He felt a real connection and was looking for ways to meet her outside of the work setting. One day Lady Luck took up his cause.

There was a local skating rink that they both frequented on weekends. One Saturday Fran was the last person on the end of a human whip of skaters racing around the rink. Try as she might, she could not keep up with the fast pace, lost her grip and went hurtling across the ice into the arms of a stunned but delighted young man. Art took advantage of the gift he received to properly introduce himself and offer to accompany her home. They walked and talked that blustery winter-grey afternoon and again and again into the spring.

Soon they were meeting regularly, even daily when possible. In the warmer summer evenings they sat together for hours on the front steps of one house or the other, only doors apart. Some Saturday nights they joined the kitchen dancing parties at Fran's Mom's boarding house. With him stretching to six foot one and a half and her stretching to reach five foot nothing, they cut quite a picture. On Sundays in winter they could often be found skating together at the rink, where the "Skaters 'Waltz" had become their song. Their relationship was becoming serious.

Fran was the younger of two Keane girls, daughters of Peter and Annie Mc Dermott-Keane. Art described Annie as a lovely woman in every way. Both parents were born in Ireland; Peter in Galway, Annie in the midlands of Roscommon. Tragically, Fran's Dad died of pneumonia when she was but nine months old. He had a heavy cold that fateful day as he went off to work at the railroad. It was 1915, penicillin was unknown and very few homes had phones. By the time the news reached Annie that Peter had collapsed at work, he was already at the Boston City Hospital. She arranged care for her young girls, and then raced into the city as quickly as she could. Sadly, she arrived too late to be with her husband when he died. Peter was 27. Annie, only a year younger, was now alone with her profound grief plus two small children to comfort and care for. Her own parents never crossed from Ireland. Her relationship with Peter's parents, who did live in a section of Boston, had never really developed as a daughter-in-law might hope. Annie was pretty much on her own.

She knew she had to find a job. What she could do to earn a living was a whole other question. Back in Ireland she had been an excellent seamstress, even winning a sewing contest. The prize was a brand new Singer sewing machine which she promptly sold, bought passage, and began her journey to America. She decided that sewing was it. She would search for work where she could put her innate skills to a financial end.

Fortunately, she soon was hired at the Reese Button Machine Company, a place where Fran herself later worked for awhile before she got married. Annie never re-married but there were some men in her life over the years. They were the male boarders she took in to supplement her salary and help ends meet. The decision to have boarders was not made lightly. It came from necessity and meant that her daughters were a vital part of her plan. They had to learn quite young how to clean, cook and keep a house since their Mother was off to work early each morning. They were latch-key kids, coming home from school, letting themselves in and doing their chores before their mother arrived to prepare the evening meal. Fran grew up used to hard work, knowing fairly young how to manage a full household and how to make every available dollar stretch to its limits.

It was the nineteen-thirties. The powerful effects from the stock market crash had penetrated everywhere, changing the fabric of most people's lives, some drastically. Bread lines, soup kitchens, tent cities even in the sub-zero conditions of winter were scenes too common across the nation. The ranks of the new poor were bulging with millions of men, women and children with hollow cheeks and empty stomachs.

By the time Franklin Delano Roosevelt first became the President in 1932, he knew the nation sorely needed some glimmers of hope. People had to believe that a day would come when they might again be able to earn decent money with some regularity; feed their family and have a decent place to live. Roosevelt calculated that the country's business sector would not, in reality could not, rebound from the situation on its own. Something more was needed. Through his Fireside Chats, which became "required" household radio listening across the nation, President Roosevelt encouraged and attempted to inspire the American people. He spoke to them regularly, in clear, straight talk that the average person could understand. Among his many important messages to the American people was his conviction that they had "...nothing to fear but fear itself."

Fully aware that people needed more than political rhetoric, Roosevelt introduced into Congress a series of public works programs (WPA) that would eventually employ hundreds of thousands of ordinary citizens. This helped people to begin to believe, not just that they would survive this, but that gradually they could get something of their normal lives back. Their families, their bruised and battered lives had some possibility of eventual relief.

Being employed by the WPA was considered by Art to be his first real job after graduation from high school. He was hired to help pave the avenue in front of the Carney Hospital in

Dorchester. Later when that had run its course, Bill Carey, a Boston City Councilor, also an usher in the center aisle at Mission Church, succeeded in getting Art a second WPA job. This one involved delivering ninety-eight pound bags of potatoes to designated drop off points around the city where needy people could go to collect food. The driver of the truck had his own ideas of how the deliveries were to be done. He had his own definite daily priorities. The first delivery of his route was to the local barroom. The workers delivered the potatoes out back while the driver downed one, two, or maybe even a third ten- cent beer. Only when this thirst-quenching ritual was completed did they move on to make deliveries to the rest of the food stations around the city. Once in passing through the streets of downtown Boston, all traffic was brought to a prolonged stop. Getting down to inquire about the cause of the delay, Art caught sight of a motorcade and of President Roosevelt being driven up State Street toward the Capitol.

This work was okay for a time, pay was not bad, but it had no future whatsoever and Art knew that. When there was an opening at Rexall Drug Company he applied, working in the print shop cutting boxes and making labels for medicines. Again, it was all right but had no permanence. He made a little more money so he could begin to put a few dollars away. The big drawback at Rexall was that the work level he was at did not have much in terms of advancement. Finally, one fine day came what he considered the chance of a lifetime. He got the green light to apply to work for the American Telephone and Telegraph Company, known commonly as AT&T.

With AT&T, at that time, there was an operational setup whereby an employee could work his way up the proverbial ladder from outside lineman to inside repairman, to third lineman, even into management. This was exactly the chance that Art wanted. He interviewed well, was hired and from then on, a forty-year mutually beneficial working relationship with the American Telephone and Telegraph Corporation began.

During the mid to late thirties, his early years with AT&T, there were several painful layoffs, but with a foot in the door, Art was not about to give up on the company. He found temporary jobs, like working at a local brewery in 1938, staying there only until the telephone company sent out the word that they were re-hiring workers. He was right back as soon as the call came. He found the work challenging on many levels and valued the community-like atmosphere in the work place. There was hope for a good future here and he was determined to work hard and be ready as each door opened.

Having secured better employment Art was able, the following year, to close a deal on a second-hand car, a Ford, complete with a running board. He paid a total of $110.00 to its former owner, who requested a check for $100.00 and ten dollars in cash. When asked about this arrangement, the man smiled slyly admitting that the check would go directly to the wife and the other ten directly into his own pocket.

With a decent job that held the promise of some economic security, Art began to dream about proposing to Fran. He knew he was ready, but he was not fully sure if she was. Fran was then twenty years of age.

On the afternoon of the day that he had chosen for the proposal, the sun shone beautifully. The sky was a brilliant almost cloudless clear blue. He and Fran went walking together. They were passing through a quiet tree lined area of the Fenway close to the river, when they paused just to enjoy the beauty. Art grew silent for a moment, then summoning up his courage, he leaned toward Fran and asked her if she would marry him. Her face softened, her eyes glowed. After what seemed like a forever, she firmly and simply responded, "Yes, I will."

There was tremendous excitement when Art and Fran announced their engagement, especially since it would be the very first wedding of their generation on either side of the families. Wedding planning began in earnest. The date chosen was April 30, 1935.

The last day of April dawned with ominously overcast skies. Heavy black-bottomed rain clouds hung darkly over the city. There would be no sunshine that day. By the time Fran's family drove the short distance to the church and Fran stepped out of the car to dash across the wide plaza toward Mission Church, the heavens had opened wide. The rain was persistent, intense, forceful, literally dancing in the streets. Mary, Fran's older sister, picked up the train of Fran's wedding gown as they raced across the pavement, up the stairs and into the back of the church, where they vigorously shook the raindrops from their clothing.

The warm glow of the brightly lit interior of the church full of friends, neighbors and loved ones almost instantly erased anything of the world outside. Softly at first, then more forcefully, the organ came alive, sending strains of music reverberating through the length and breadth of Mission Church. Fran beamed as she moved slowly down the broad middle aisle toward the altar. Looking handsome in his dark suit, Art waited by the bottom step near the altar rail, eager to receive her hand in his. From now on they would fully belong to one another as husband and wife "...till death do us part." Nothing, but nothing could dampen their spirits that day.

After the beautiful wedding ceremony, the guests were invited back to the reception at Mrs. Keane's house. Tables were laden with trays of delicious foods; musicians played, dancers whirled. The rooms filled with laughter and good natured talk. Everyone was enjoying the celebration. Their parents, Catherine, Annie and even James beamed as they watched their grown-up, newly married kids. They could hardly believe how swiftly the years had flown.

Finally, after several wonderful hours together with their guests, the newlyweds packed up the borrowed car which had recently been offered by concerned relatives who were not totally confident that Art's car could safely make a long trip. Amidst hugs, tears and showers of rice, Art and Fran set off for their honeymoon, heading first to Albany, New York's capital and beyond.

A Family of Their Own

78 Fenwood Road was the first place they called home in the early years of their marriage. 875 Huntington Avenue, second floor, over a grocery store was another. But once they became aware of the activities of their 'colorful' neighbors living upstairs, it did not seem wise to have Fran alone in the evenings when Art worked overtime. They continued their search.

It wasn't long after their honeymoon that Fran suspected, and then confirmed that she was pregnant. Overjoyed, they began to prepare to become parents. A few months into the pregnancy at a company picnic, a telephone worker who had too much to drink, lost his footing and fell against Fran knocking her down. As a result she suffered a miscarriage. The doctors were somewhat concerned about the effects of the accident but she was young and strong, although slight, weighing only eighty some pounds. Within the very next year she was pregnant again. With confidence she and Art looked forward not back. They hoped and prayed for a healthy newborn.

It was late April. The fresh fragrant scents of spring had begun to fill the air. Their first wedding anniversary was approaching. Fran was definitely showing. The baby was due in mid-July. Since this was to be the first grandchild ever for both families, there was lots of excitement as the time drew closer. Some of Art's siblings were still in their teens, so being an uncle or an aunt was a big deal.

Mrs. Keane asked Art and Fran to drop over to see her the eve of their anniversary. Before they left her house she went into her bedroom, brought out a brightly wrapped box and gave them their anniversary gift. Fran protested that they would come by again tomorrow, but her mother quietly insisted they take the present along with them now. That seemed strange but they did not give it any more thought until early the next morning when a neighbor began rapping loudly on their apartment door, urging them to come with her and come at once. It was April 30, 1936.

Entering Mrs. Keane's home, they found Fran's mother, who had suffered a severe heart attack, lying pale and limp on her bed, unable to even move by her own power. Dr. John Adams, the family physician, worked quietly at the bedside giving her something which calmed her considerably. He rose, took them aside and in a soft, low voice explained that medically, there was nothing more that he could offer her. The attack had been massive. He marveled that she was still alive at all. Moving her to the hospital would serve no purpose. She was better here among loved ones.

He reached out and squeezed Fran's hand caringly. His face was deeply lined with compassion and sorrow. Annie had been his patient for many years now. Then, he excused himself to finish his visits, promising to return as soon as his work would allow.

When he entered the room a few hours later, some of Annie's friends fingered their beads, praying in low murmurs. After checking her vitals, the doctor gave her another injection, then moving into the one empty straight back chair near her bed, continued to monitor her slowing breathing. After a while he again took his leave, telling them that it was a matter of time, very little time at that.

Fran and her sister, Mary sat close to their mother, stroking her hand, cooling her brow with a wet cloth or joining in the prayers of neighbors who quietly slipped in and out of the room as the day wore on. Tears filled their eyes as Mary and Fran, each whispered final words into their mother's ear. Art remained close by, silently accompanying Fran as she reluctantly loved her mother into eternity.

Dr. Adams returned from his day's work, a very short time after Annie had breathed her last. The undertaker had been called. The room was slowly emptying out. Annie's daughters had not moved at all. After what he judged a respectful amount of time, he gently approached Fran. Knowing of her past miscarriage, he strongly urged her to go home and try to get some rest. She was almost seven months pregnant and it had been a very long painful day. For the sake of her baby she needed to be careful. Fran reluctantly acquiesced. She was totally drained. Words would not come, just waves of sorrow. She let Art help her into her coat. Sitting down once more by the bed, she kissed her mother's forehead, hugged her sister and the faithful friends still gathered, then left.

She slept sparingly, even fitfully that night. So many thoughts and feelings swept through her. Her mother, the only parent she had ever known, was suddenly gone. She would never cradle or bless their first grandchild, nor be there to encourage her youngest daughter, or to calm her fears. Who would Fran turn to now when she was worried, when her child became ill, or when that first tooth was coming? Tears fell.

Over the next months of the pregnancy, Art and Fran grew closer, giving hope and strength to one another.

The day of rejoicing came July 16, 1936 when their healthy baby boy came into the world. They could hardly contain themselves. Fran had never had a brother, had never really known her father. How utterly precious it was for her to hold her son, Arthur Thomas Jr., while being held by her husband who just sat near her, smiling broadly as family members came and went for the whole day.

A short time after the baby's birth a flat in a house at 192 Hillside Street came available, so they moved 'up the hill,' as the expression went. Finally, life seemed to be taking on a rhythm of its own. Soon Fran became pregnant again, but it was apparent very early on in the pregnancy that things were not going well. Dr. Gorman, her obstetrician, became concerned and brought her into the hospital for observation in her fifth month. Serious complications developed rather quickly. Fran came close to losing her life during the miscarriage. Years later, while watching a talk show where guests were sharing "life after death" experiences, she spoke about a memory of what happened at the time of this miscarriage. She said that she knew she was in the hospital, but suddenly she felt she was being transported to a lovely, warm, sunny, open space where many of her loved ones surrounded her. It was so peaceful there. She felt no fears whatsoever, just peace. Then suddenly, she could hear her name being called loudly and insistently. She truly felt pulled in two directions until somehow she remembered making a real conscious choice to leave this beautiful place, follow the voice that was calling her and to go back. At some deep level, the sense of well-being that enveloped her throughout that whole experience influenced her approach to serious illness and death ever after.

Just a little over a year after that loss, on June 30, 1938, Art and Fran welcomed a baby girl named Joan Claire, who weighed in at six pounds, fifteen ounces. Given Fran's recent miscarriage, Dr. Gorman had carefully scheduled this baby's arrival. He was taking absolutely no chances. He brought Fran into St. Elizabeth's Hospital early that morning inducing her labor, feeling it was crucial to monitor all aspects of this delivery with extreme care. Baby Joan squawked her way into life mid-afternoon of that sultry summer day, around 2:30 p.m. Little did Art and Fran realize as they cuddled their girl, that she was the first of seven daughters who would grace the family over the next twenty years: (Barbara (1941), Nancy (1944), Mary (1948), Carol (1949), Claire (1953) and Debra (1958).

Art and Fran had hoped for another boy, but when Debbie was born, Fran, believing this to be her last pregnancy, decided to simply give her baby girl a name with special initials, D.A.D.-Debra Ann Doyle.

That September of 1938 a powerful, blustery hurricane churned wildly through the Boston area. Most workers were let go early in order to get home safely to their families. Art caught the trolley, arriving at Brigham Circle where the buffeting winds made ordinary walking almost impossible. He turned up his collar, leaning into the fierce gusts as he struggled unsteadily up the hill. The storm was gathering force. High winds battered rooftops, sending anything not securely tied down whirling dangerously off into space. When he finally entered his house he found Art Jr. cautiously peeking out under the tightly drawn shades of the living room window, while Fran sat protectively in the corner of the room clutching the baby, unsure what to expect next. Relief flooded her whole being when Art tumbled through the door exhausted from the sheer effort of the climb. Winds howled on unabated throughout the entire night. Only gradually during the following days did they realize the full extent of the devastation that was wrought by the storm through different areas of the city, as well as up and down the eastern coastline.

During the end of 1930s into the 40s, one of the WPA construction jobs undertaken in the city was the building of low income housing units in the Roxbury area of Boston between the Art Museum on Huntington Avenue and Mission Grammar School. The Projects, as they were called, were three -story reddish brick structures with varying sized apartments in different buildings. Several such apartment set-ups were attached forming a block. In between each block was an open area for kids to play; space with clothes lines for wash and a parking lot for those fortunate enough to own a car.

Kids abounded, an average family having three or four, with perhaps another on the way. There was no need to search for playmates. They came in abundance, all ages and sizes. Older kids wandered up to the more spacious athletic fields near the church. Younger ones played on the blacktop out back, swung on the swings or climbed jungle bars under the watchful eyes of their own Mom or a few moms of the neighborhood who all seemed to have the same book of do's and don'ts for children. Although some mothers joined the work force during the 1940s as part of the war effort, the majority of them were full-time, stay at home, moms.

The Projects, in the early 1940s, was a safe, community-minded place to live and to bring up kids.

No one had a lot of worldly goods, but they had each other and were ready and willing to be there for one another in good times and rough ones, which eventually came to everyone. Most families were blue-collar workers of Irish-Catholic descent. In fine weather some of the local men sat outside on the front steps of the apartment buildings in the evening, reading the paper, solving the world's problems, telling war stories and keeping an eye on the kids, while their wives tidied up inside after supper. If it were during the school year, the kids went in early to do homework then headed off to bed. In the summer this eased up and most kids stayed out at least until the street lights went on. Then one could count on seeing different mothers' heads, one by one, appearing at the windows above the front steps. Each had her own distinctive way of calling her children. No message was really needed beyond the recognizable recitation of the names. The kids knew the rest of the routine.

Throughout the summer the city of Boston hired youth workers who provided programs to fill the vacation time for the neighborhood kids. Most activities took place up the park. The workers taught crafts, played board games and organized team sports for girls and boys of varied age groups. At the end of these days, most youngsters simply tumbled into bed with no fuss at all; their energy well spent racing, competing or just horsing around with friends. Sometimes, groups got together from different areas of Boston. Often the youth workers organized cross city events and sectional competitions. The annual Fourth of July celebration was usually the spectacular event. There might be music, games with prizes, some version of a cook-out and then the holiday might end with an outdoor movie after dark, accompanied by hot popcorn or ice cream treats. Life was good for kids those years.

When Art and Fran first married they spoke of their marriage as a partnership. They wanted to raise the family together. In living this out, Art proved himself a man ahead of his time, sharing in some of the household chores, including the care of the kids. He could sort of defend himself in the kitchen. He was basically a meat and potato man who classified most other culinary options, especially culturally different foods with strong seasonings, as "queer food". Experimenting with these latter tastes was simply not done willingly, if at all. One exception was basic Chinese fare, which he eventually grew to really appreciate and enjoy. Generally though, he favored the tried and true and faithfully stuck by them all his life. He and Fran each had a highly developed sweet tooth which they passed along as part of the family gene pool.

They were active Catholics, whose faith shaped their everyday lives, influencing their family values. They wanted each child to feel loved and accepted for who he or she was. Early on they made a pact to help one another not play favorites.

A sound education was another concern. Art and Fran had high school diplomas, but knew that the next generation would need more than that to make it. But besides book learning, they saw to it that the kids had chances to learn life lessons that can't be taught per se. Some of these came from the people who came to the house, or whom the family visited or just met by chance; from experiences both joyful and pain-filled, from choices; from just engaging everyday life fully and pondering what it said to you. Sometimes after an event, like when Mary had to testify in court after a car accident, Art would exclaim about what a great opportunity it was, "You couldn't buy that kind of learning."

He enjoyed life, drinking deeply of the varied flavors it offered. He wanted his kids to do the same.

They instilled the value of an honest days' work, of integrity, humor, of giving back to the community, of loving faithfully and being there for others, especially for family. Seldom, if ever, did they speak about these things. They simply lived their lives that way.

They were great for adventures like trips to Franklin Park Zoo, the Art Museum, picnicking, walking the historic streets of Boston (later called the Freedom Trail), and showing up at any parade within earshot. Even a car ride was full of games: identifying license plates, shouting a state / guessing the capital, Name That Tune and more. Keeping kids entertained while traveling was honed to a fine art.

Early on, Art bought a 1930 Ford, running board and all. Thank God for that the day his oldest daughter, Joanie, sat in the front seat with her younger sister, Barbie, waiting for their Dad. Having nothing to do and being of a curious bent, Joanie began to fiddle with the interesting looking stick in between the front seats. After a few tugs she successfully loosened it, causing the car to begin slowly rolling down the sloping incline of the street, picking up momentum as it did. A neighbor shrieked to Art who came dashing out of the first floor apartment, leaped onto the running board and yanked the shift stick back so firmly it almost came out of the floor. The car came to a screeching, bumpy halt. The two kids looked terrified. No one spoke for what seemed like five minutes. Thoughts of what could have happened sent Art's heart racing for days

Because Art worked for the Telephone Company, the family had a four, then a two-party phone line which was great, but also a challenge. In the early days of telephones in private homes, normally no one rang just to pass the time of day. If someone called it was to announce a birth, an engagement, serious illness or death. Art and Fran had the only phone among the six families at 655 Parker Street. It was not uncommon, especially on weekends, to have neighbors around the kitchen table any hour of the day or even the night, waiting to use the phone or to receive a call, Fran might be ironing clothes or preparing a meal, but she simply put on the kettle and settled in. The neighbor could be exuberantly sharing news celebrating the birth of a new niece or shedding tears because a loved one was ill. Tea cups came out, sweets appeared. Talking might change nothing whatsoever of the situation, yet somehow the sharing, the sitting down together seemed to help. More than once Art drove someone to the hospital when a relative was seriously ill or dying. Depending on the day or the hour, he might lump one or two young ones into the back seat, so Fran had some moments of peace and quiet back at home.

They lived within walking distance of both the church and local Catholic school. Each child, when of age, was registered at Mission Grammar School. The kids wandered home for lunch and were back in the school yard playing before the bell rang for afternoon classes. There was no tuition in those days, but Art and Fran got involved in the fund raising activities of the parish community. They, with the kids, could be found at every bazaar or cake sale held. They bought play or concert tickets, Christmas cards, candy bars, with whatever they could spare from the week's paycheck envelopes. Between these activities, processions, services at church, visits from the Redemptorist priests, band rehearsals, orchestra practice, homework, and sporting events, their days were full.

It was in many ways a child centered home, yet Art and Fran kept up old friendships, enjoyed adult parish activities and regularly carved out time together for a movie or some simple thing away from the house. Art was lucky to have his younger sister Anne and her girlfriends to call upon as trusted baby-sitters for an evening out.

As the family grew, so did expenses. To supplement his day job, Art, who had played basketball in high school, became a basketball referee for the many colleges and high schools in the surrounding area. On game night he arrived from work, had supper, donned his freshly-ironed black and white striped referee shirt and was off. If it were not a school night, a few of the older ones might go with him. The cheering of the crowds and the fast pace of the game were exciting, that is, until the referee made a call that was unpopular with the crowd. Immediately they were on their feet yelling vociferously, "Kill the referee!" The atmosphere was electrically charged. Chills ran down the kids' spines. Ordinarily, after a moment or so, Art blew his whistle, announced the penalty and called for resumption of playing, allowing the mood to shift, the action to continue and his kids to breathe a major sigh of relief.

Art and Fran would help the kids with home work and reasonably good grades were definitely expected when report cards came. No one had to have all A's, but each one needed to do his/her level best. Once when Art was on an assignment in a downtown bank installing their phone system, he noticed a sign on each manager's desk that said only one word, THINK. Seeing this as a great motivator, he procured one and ensconced it on the top of the refrigerator.

At Mission, once any student reached third grade, it was possible to begin music lessons. To Art and Fran that seemed like a great opportunity, so when the time came, each child was signed up to play a musical instrument. Where they ever unearthed the instruments was a mystery, but at the appointed time, the instruments appeared. Art Jr. played the trumpet, Joanie the violin (and was a majorette in the band), Barb, the clarinet. Then the chain broke. Nancy had rheumatic fever as a child and had enough to do to keep up with her studies.

From that time onward the piano became the instrument of choice, but neither Mary, nor Carol nor Debbie ever mastered it. Claire had innate talent, but she was obviously quite gifted artistically. Art lessons won out in the end. It was Art himself who had an ear for music. He could sit down at a piano and make it talk. Someone hummed the melody, within minutes he found the notes, added chords and everyone could sing along.

Art loved everything about the ocean, the sun, the sand and the cooler evening breezes. As his family grew he got creative about how to have regular dips in the Atlantic. Many a summer night, after supper, he loaded the kids into the car and drove the short distance to Carson Beach in Southie. It helped use up lots of energy, gave Fran a rest and let him enjoy a swim plus time with the kids.

Although money was often tight, Art and Fran usually found ways to take the family out of the city for a break during the summer. It might just be a walk around Jamaica Pond, or an almost spontaneous overnight trip to a friend in New York or day trips to Nantasket beach. A few summers they managed to share costs for a cottage near the beach at Nantasket or Manomet or in New Hampshire with a relative or a friend from work. The quarters might have been tight or noisy, but those summer vacations hold great memories for everyone.

To live in one of the apartments within the Projects, a tenant had to earn under a specified salary level. To Art's joy, then chagrin, he received notice at work of a coming raise in pay, one, he soon realized, that would put him just a tad above that listed amount. He knew with six kids he was unable to afford housing anywhere else at that time, so he had to make the unprecedented request at work not to receive the raise until he could figure out what to do next about housing for his family.

Whether fate or coincidence, it happened that at that time Fran's Aunt Catherine was in financial straits. She owned an old triple-decker on 65 Hillside Street that she was about to lose unless she could find a buyer. The house was not in the greatest condition but was large enough for his family and with work, had possibilities. Art and Fran considered the whole situation, and then they decided to take the leap and buy the house. There was one big issue on the practical side. Art did not have on hand the more than $100.00 up front for passing the papers, so he approached his insurance broker, J. F. Clune, who listened to his plan, then lent him the money directly. Within weeks the papers were signed, they got the house, moved the family in, and Art accepted the promised raise. He and Fran proudly became first time home owners.

To show his gratitude for the loan, Art remained a loyal customer with J.F. Clune Insurance as long as Mr. Clune was in business, even after Art moved thirty miles away.

At a family party several months after this purchase, while some old songs were being belted out somewhat off key, someone asked, "Does anyone know *A Shanty in Old Shanty Town*? Without missing a beat Art replied, "Not only do I know it. I now own it!"

The Years Rolled By

By now Art had been with the New England branch of the AT&T Company for more than twenty years. He found it a great place to work, one where both management and staff looked out for each other. If someone began to hit the bottle, his buddies tried to straighten him out. If a worker got seriously ill or injured, the company would do whatever was possible to help the family through it. There was a sense of being part of a common effort. They worked together, shared together and celebrated together whenever possible. One year on a significant birthday, Art's co-workers bought him a luscious cake which they had their taste buds ready to enjoy with him at lunch time. He looked at the cake with its thick chocolate frosting, smiled his approval at their choice, then thanking them profusely, he carefully tucked the layered cake back into its box, saying to his dismayed co-workers, "My kids will love this cake tonight after supper."

During the earlier years of their marriage, it had not always been easy to work, be with Fran and the kids, referee when possible, plus do the studying necessary to pass the different exams by which Art knew he could get ahead in the telephone company. He had done it, though, and had advanced, earning a strong hands-on grasp of operational skills. Now as he observed varied internal changes and felt the pulse of the telephone business itself, he realized that he needed to do more to improve his educational background, since he sorely lacked the academic credentials now being sought. He had to find a way to go back to school, to college, at night. Working it out with Fran, he began taking courses part-time at Northeastern University in both English and Business. Most of his fellow students were about half his age, but he didn't let that stop him. He persevered. Actually, he thrived on the challenges and within just over two years he earned an Associate degree.

He was on a roll. Although he was a good communicator he decided, in the late 1950s to sign up for a Dale Carnegie course, *Effective Speaking, Leadership Training and Human Relations.* The full extent of what was mastered in this enterprise will never be known, but ask any of his kids what he learned and they will launch into the mantra that became a family legend. He came home determined not to be one of "the men in the ranks." Apparently Mr. Carnegie more than once declared,

> "I know men in the ranks, who will stay in the ranks.
> WHY?
> I'll tell you why,
> simply because...
> they don't have the ability to get the job done."

The last line was typically delivered with the wallop of a tightly rolled newspaper against the back of the kitchen chair. A sense of responsibility was important. If you took on a job, especially one that involved others' lives, he expected you to see it through until it was done and done as well as possible.

In the early '60s he signed into the Archdiocesan Labor Institute, eventually receiving a certificate in Labor Relations. He knew that openings were coming in management. He was determined to be ready to step up to the plate.

Within the telephone company work force, Art was a Union shop steward, a staunch defender of what he believed to be right. For three or four years running, he served on the Executive Committee of the International Brotherhood of Telephone Workers: Local 2. He got a real shock one time, after a pretty stormy Union meeting where he faced down Tim Murphy, one of his bosses who had lived on the second floor on 20 Francis Street when Art was a teen-ager. Later that week, when they were alone, Tim told Art that he would never have even gotten an interview for the telephone company without his help. Tim had been the one who put in a good word, opening up that door for him and he did not appreciate how this favor was being returned. Art was totally floored by this news, having always believed that another person had gotten him the green light.

During these years, Richard Cushing was Archbishop, then Cardinal, of the Boston Archdiocese. He was a generous prelate who kept touch not only with the needs of the people of his large flock, but his pastoral concerns widened to include mission countries of the world. To fund these projects he asked Catholics in parishes, schools, and the work force to donate something on a regular basis. When Art began at A T &T, a quarter was collected each Thursday, payday, for the Cardinal's fund. When the older worker who collected the money retired, he asked Arthur to organize these donations in the future. He did just that for all the years that Cardinal Cushing remained active in Boston.

Not surprisingly, given Art's Irish background, he had an avid interest in politics at all levels. If he believed in the values of a local candidate, he supported him or even her whenever possible, getting his children involved too. When Kathleen Ryan Dacey, a Mission Hill lawyer, decided to run for the Boston City Council, Art worked at her headquarters making calls and arranging transportation for older voters. His kids wrote and sent postcards to long lists of local constituents. On voting day, rain or shine, they would be outside a heavily populated polling place handing out leaflets. Kathleen, who won on more than one occasion, never forgot the support that Art gave her. She, in turn, was there for him when some real legal needs arose not many years later.

One of those times came around in the early nineteen fifties. Art and Fran were driving home from an early evening movie. They saw something in the road ahead that looked very much like a body. Braking quickly, they got out to investigate further. With a quick check they realized that the man lying there was drunk and somewhat injured. He must have fallen off the curb, was hurt and unable to stand on his own. They felt they could not just drive away and leave him there lying in the street. Art looked the man over again and seeing nothing that seemed like a serious injury, decided to at least pull the man over to the sidewalk, out of harm's way. Then he would call the police. While Art bent over, putting his arms under the man's shoulders to begin to move him, a second car pulled up and the driver, an influential man in the local community, jumped out and began shouting orders in all directions. Without asking Art or Fran anything, he made the assumption that they had hit the man and now were trying to destroy evidence by clearing things up.

As the accusations flew, a small crowd began to gather. Someone quickly went to the phone booth nearby and called the local police in Brighton. Before Art and Fran clearly knew what was happening around them, they were officially accused of a hit and run accident. Within days they received in the mail a summons to appear in Brighton District Court for arraignment. The charges were quite serious. If Art were to be found guilty, he could find himself in jail.

The mood in the Doyle household was very tense as they prepared for the Court appearances. It became a jury trial in the end and was not looking good. A dent was found in the right side of their car, at just about the height where it might match the man's injuries. They were beside themselves with worry about the verdict as well as the mounting costs involved. Besides their vacation fund, they were eating into their scant savings. They knew they were innocent but that was hardly enough. While their lawyer was doing everything possible, they stormed heaven for help. It finally came one evening as they were pouring over some family albums. Before their eyes they saw a photo taken over a year earlier which clearly showed Art's younger twin brothers standing alongside the car which already, one year ago, had the infamous dent. That was exactly what was needed to break the case wide open, set them free and let them breathe deeply once more. The verdict was delivered in their favor. The case was closed. They could pick up their lives once again, that is once they lit one more candle at the Shrine, this time in thanksgiving.

Cars and driving were soon to be in Art's life in another way. The kids were reaching the age when learning to drive became a focus, even an obsession in their lives. There was no course called *Driver's Education* when Art Jr. reached 16, so he looked to his Dad to fill the bill. Now, Art, Sr. had already tried this role once before, without great success. His father had never learned to drive a car on his own, but did have experience "driving" a boat from his years in the service. He asked his son to teach him to drive, quite convinced that his skills were transferable. Art did his best over a few months, only gradually discovering the built-in challenge. As you operate a boat you turn the wheel round to the left to head the boat to the right, and to the right to have the boat turn left, precisely the opposite of driving a car. After many lessons Art's father felt he had it down pat, so he made an appointment for the road test.

All was moving along just fine as the elder Mr. Doyle and the examiner were heading up from the fish pier in downtown Boston on the way back toward the police station. The license was almost a sure thing. Suddenly there was a shift in the traffic pattern, a real distraction and wham, the old habits kicked right in. Being directed to take a right turn, he pulled the wheel hard all the way around to the left, right into the opposite lane of traffic. "STOP" the examiner commanded, panic in his voice. Test finished, story over. Art's Dad never tried for his license again.

Each one of his teenagers naturally came at this learning how to drive experience differently, varying with their personalities. Fran had never gotten her license and worried out loud as each one of the kids began this journey toward a new kind of independence. Art found being the family driving instructor quite stressful. The kids' lives were in his hands as well as the lives of whoever else was on the road. He felt keenly responsible that the kids drive carefully. He wanted them to know the rules; drive at sensible speeds; make mature decisions; and do it all at just sixteen years of age or younger, depending on when they got a permit.. He tried to pour all his years of experience behind the wheel into each one of them quickly, beginning with day one of seating them behind the wheel of the car. He knew at some level that he could not really do that, but that did nothing to stop him from trying and trying hard. His kids remarked that it was like Clark Kent (Superman) stepping into a phone booth and coming out a different person. This usually mild- mannered man could suddenly become a terror as a driving instructor.

With one of his children, after several tension-wrought tries, they mutually decided that Driver Education classes were called for and right away. Gratefully high schools had begun to offer such courses as the years went by. With his eighth student, Debbie, just one afternoon's experience of driving lessons sent her scrambling after Mike Grady, her sister Claire's boyfriend, who had been driving for a few years. She jabbered at him incessantly until she convinced Mike that he was the chosen one teaching her to drive. She sheepishly thanked her Dad for his valiant efforts. They then went their separate ways, gladly.

At Home in Braintree

For years Art had dreamed of finding a place to live just outside the city. One day during lunch on the job, a co-worker, Johnny Davey, told him about a house for sale diagonally across the street from him in a town called Braintree, right off Route 3 South. Art talked with Fran. They were interested, so a showing was arranged. Once they saw the deep red two- story wood framed house at 175 Hollingsworth Avenue and toured every room inside, they knew that they wanted it. There was a good sized cellar, a driveway, a garage, and a yard in the back. Behind the house, which was on the corner of Hollingsworth and Oak Hill Road, were trees stretching up a gently sloping hill. From what they could pick up from a few neighbors around, it seemed a friendly area with younger families. There was space for additional homes to be built, for new families to arrive. In fact Johnny told them that there were contracting plans before the Town Board to begin building new homes on Oak Hill shortly.

Having found the house they wanted, the next step was securing the down- payment. They applied to the telephone company for a loan. When the AT&T representative came out to assess the house, he looked through every room on both floors, plus the unfinished basement. He asked many questions, then retired to his car where he sat and sat for what seemed like ages. Art and Fran were inside sitting on crates, nervously wondering what was going on. Almost one full hour later the agent rang the doorbell, came inside and told them he would approve the loan for $8,000.00. They were thrilled. They were going to have their little patch in the suburbs, which felt wonderful. They were also nervous knowing they were making a big financial commitment here. They had to weigh out the realities that they had not yet completed the sale of their house on Hillside Street, and off and on lately, their car had been on the fritz. They knew they were going to walk a tight financial rope for a long stretch, but they wanted their kids to live in the “country.” They put all these very real concerns out of their minds for the night. They just wanted to enjoy the wonder of it all and believe it would work out. From 1956 when they purchased the house until 2005 when it was finally sold, just before the housing bust, the family lived, grew and thrived in this home.

Once they owned the house they began to shape it to their needs and tastes. There were seven children and two adults at that time, with only three rooms upstairs. The first change was to convert the dining room into Art and Fran’s bedroom, where fortunately their furniture fit snugly. Upstairs, one bedroom became Arthur’s and the other two, including the spacious master bedroom, were for the girls. A year and a half later, in 1958, their seventh and last daughter joined the family, spending months in her crib downstairs and then finally joining the Doyle girls’ dorm on the second floor.

Next, Art wanted a fence for the back yard so that the youngest kids could play outside safely. Once that was in place, he envisioned a walk-way from the back door to the garage, plus a small stone fireplace outside. For these projects he needed sand and stones. Where he worked downtown several buildings had been demolished. Cobblestone streets were being torn up. Reusable bricks and stones were lying around the empty lot right next door to Art's installation assignment. In conversation with the job foreman he learned that the stones and sand could be carted away at will. Art pondered this opportunity figuring out a plan of how to transport the materials. Before it could be executed Arthur Jr. came to him one day asking to borrow the station wagon to take his girl friend on a date. Art considered the request alongside his own needs, and struck a bargain. His son could have the car if he would pick up a load of sand and stones on his way home later that evening. It was an easy deal.

No one knows whether the girl friend was or was not a part of the evening adventure. They only knew that the bricks were delivered, the sidewalk was completed, the brick fireplace built and Art Sr. was pleased.

Art and Fran continued to enjoy an evening out together now and then. Their older kids had, over the years, grown into being their built-in baby sitters. Once when Barb and Nancy were the oldest ones still at home, Art and Fran left the house one evening for an early movie in Quincy. They made sure that the youngest, Claire, was already bathed and fully ready for bed. Before they set off, last minute do's and don'ts were clearly spelled out. It was a lovely, absolutely cloudless early fall Friday evening, one made for being outdoors. About halfway through the drive to the movie theater, Fran interrupted her conversation with Art to say that she had forgotten something and needed to stop back at the house. She could just run in, pick it up and be out in a minute. Art did a quick U-turn and headed back.

On the home front, expecting their parents to be gone for at least two hours or more, Nancy had called her friend, Frani, and was happily biking along toward Thayer Academy to meet her (one of the expressed don'ts). Barb was leisurely chatting on the phone while blowing firmly shaped smoke rings that floated lazily out the basement window. Claire had joined some of the younger Davey kids making mud pies in the grassy median strip, while managing to wear much of it. Mary and Carol were stretched out on the front steps in their pjs, fully engrossed in listening to the latest hit tunes.

When Art turned the car onto the street next to Thayer Academy, Nancy, Frani and the bikes were right in their path. There was no escape. Nancy recognized immediately that she was in big trouble, but decided to try to warn the others. With the words "Get home now" ringing in her ears, she began pedaling as fast as her legs would carry her through the shortcut up toward the house. She arrived just in time to watch their car sweep into the driveway where they had a panoramic view of everything and everyone around. The kids only needed to take one look at their parents' expressions. Not much was said, nor was it needed.

Within the telephone company, Art was promoted to a managerial position and transferred to the new office floor that AT&T opened at the Prudential Building in Boston. Braintree to in-town Boston was, depending on the traffic at any given time, about a half hour to an hour trip each day. Gas plus parking fees were expensive, so Art, considering that he drove a station wagon in to work each day anyhow, offered to car pool. He figured it was a win-win situation. It would help some co-workers arrive at work more easily, while also covering basic expenses.

The years at the Prudential were among Art's most creative and productive ones. He had hit his stride, knew his trade very well; was seen as a bright, friendly, organized, and innovative thinker with fine management instincts.. He became known as the office problem solver. His ideas and creative work forms were highly valued. He once forwarded a sample of these to the department head explaining their potential and suggesting that the staff might fill one out for each problem situation as it arose. His custom became to sign the designated forms with only his initials, ATD. Before he left the downtown office, most problem resolution patterns or forms were referred to throughout his department simply as the ATDs.

Art had a cool head, not tending to get upset when things went awry at work. One particular day, just about all the phones in every store, office or company at the Prudential Building went dead almost simultaneously. Some folks on the AT&T floor were dashing around shouting orders at anyone who could hear them. Once Art got wind of the systems failure, he and his team set about figuring out the source of the problem as fast as their skills would allow them.

Immediately, when they fingered the trouble spot they fixed it, filed the required report form and life within the Pru hummed back into normal gear.

During the many years that Art worked downtown, he was often involved in jobs at what was simply called the jewelers building, located on Washington Street near City Hall. He had installed phones, run lines for system changes and done trouble shooting. He was well known to several dealers within the building. These relations served him well one year when he decided to make a very special purchase, one with a story behind it.

At some point, Art learned that within the first few years of their marriage, the diamond in Fran's ring came loose. One day, to her horror, she realized that it was gone, only the prongs remaining. She scoured every inch of the house frantically, looked in every purse, every pocket of her clothing, retraced her steps, but to no avail. Upset as she was, she decided it would be best to keep this as her secret, at least at that time. She replaced the missing stone with one that looked quite similar to the diamond of the original ring. Over the years, at a time known only between them, the whole true story was finally shared.

Since then, year after year, Art put away a little bit of money here and there, with the dream that one day he would replace that diamond. Many seasons came and went before he saved enough to consider buying a new ring. It was late March of 1970. Their thirty-fifth wedding anniversary was approaching. This, he decided, would be the year. Art visited the Jewelers' Building more than once over the early months of that year, finally selecting the diamond he wanted for her. When told its full price, considering the setting he chose, he knew he would have enough money for it, once one of his CDs matured. There was one big but in the way. That would only happen around the beginning of May which simply was not soon enough. He had to purchase the ring now, if he was to give it to her for their 35th wedding anniversary. A few days later when his daughter, Mary, learned of his predicament, she lent him the money. Art drove home from Boston with the small box safely tucked in his left inner jacket pocket.

The anniversary was two days away. He could hardly wait to surprise her. It was an emotional moment as Fran opened her gift. Art gently took her hand into his and for an instant they simply held one another's gaze. Then, he slipped the ring onto her finger with as much if not more love then he had 35 years before. The chemistry was still there. No words came as they embraced each other.

Then, Fran flashed a look at her hands. Without skipping a beat she moaned, "My nails are a mess!" Why didn't you warn me so I could have had a manicure? How can I show off my ring with nails like this!"

Those early years that they lived in Braintree were good ones. The younger half of the family went to the local schools in town, made life-long friends, and blossomed. Art and Fran appeared at every school function from cheer-leading, to acting to competitions of all kinds. They drove miles to be present at singing engagements where their son, Art, by himself or as one of the Three Ds, tried to make his way into the world of entertainment. Arnie Ginsberg, Dick Clark, *American Bandstand*, and the *Star of the Day* became family events. As the Three D's wrote and recorded their first original songs hopes ran high.

Art and Fran had at least one teenager in the family (sometimes two or even three) for about thirty-two years straight! Gradually, one by one, their children were becoming young adults, graduating from high school or nursing school, beginning to date seriously, finding jobs and generally starting to move toward some important personal choices about their own future lives.

Art Jr. was the first one to get married. In 1959 he wed Ann Bray. They found a home and settled in Pembroke, MA. Joanie moved to Baltimore in 1956, becoming a postulant with the School Sisters of Notre Dame. Barbie entered nursing school at the Lemuel Shattuck Hospital, a live-in experience. After becoming an LPN she married Mike Lynch, a former Marine and also moved down toward Pembroke. Nancy secured a position as a secretary at the Naval Shipyard in Quincy. Within a few years she met Jim Connor. In 1970 they began married life in their cute apartment in Quincy. Later Nancy and Jim ventured further down Route 3 south, buying a home in Kingston. August 28, 1971 Carol married John Nickerson, eventually settling into a newly built home in Plymouth.

Four or five days after Carol's wedding, Fran and Art were at home relaxing, leisurely re-playing every detail from

Saturday. They were savoring the beauty of the ceremony, the delight of family and friends, the fun everyone had at the reception, followed by the circle of good-byes as Carol and John left for their honeymoon. Carol hugged them as she left the reception hall, thanking them for a fabulous wedding, for all they had done and for their love.

Art and Fran had gone away for a few days and were only now beginning to settle back into everyday life. As they reminisced that evening, they sipped hot cups of tea while enjoying chocolate brownies and ice cream. They were so engaged in their conversation that they never heard the front door open, so were surprised when Mary and David arrived in the kitchen. They appeared to have something important to share. Mary began, her eyes bright as she told them that David had proposed to her and that she had said, "Yes". Although they had not decided on nor purchased her ring quite yet, they were officially engaged. Art and Fran congratulated them wholeheartedly with hugs all around, then asked "When were they thinking of the wedding?" There was only a slight pause before Mary continued. They were thinking of getting married this November, around Thanksgiving time, probably the Saturday after. That meant that their wedding was just three months away. Mary must have read their minds and anticipated their concerns, because she quickly went to great lengths to assure them that she knew exactly what she did and did not want for their wedding day and would organize it totally, so they need not worry about it at all. True to her word, she set about planning every detail of her wedding with David, her sisters, her girlfriends and David's family also

On a mild November morning, the twenty-seventh, Art linked his arm with Mary's at the back of St. Francis Church in Braintree, ready to walk her down the aisle. Another of his daughters was being married, another son-in-law entered the family. He kissed Mary gently as they reached the front of the church, and then placed her hand in David's. Smiling, Mary and David moved together into the sanctuary, as their wedding ceremony began.

Art and Fran now had one daughter-in-law, Ann, and four sons-in-law: Mike, Jim, John and David. Claire and Debbie were still teenagers, too young for marriage, but not too young to be babysitters and pampering aunts to their growing number of nieces and nephews.

By the early part of the seventies, AT&T opened a branch office at Braintree Plaza within a few streets of where Art lived. He was excited on one level when he was assigned there, for the long trek into Boston was over. This new location meant that some days he and Fran could even have lunch together at home. There was only one real drawback in this assignment. He came to what was called the south shore office as a relative unknown, since he had worked in various offices in and around Boston for thirty plus years. He knew no one there. They had neither personal nor professional experience of him nor his working style. It was a bit like starting over, needing to learn the ropes, getting to know people, forming working relationships and coming to be known and trusted.

When Art began in the Braintree office he was a relatively young-looking sixty year old, but as things went within companies in those days, he was definitely considered an older worker, coming close to being "over the hill." Gradually Art earned their respect and his gifts, skills and quick sense of humor were appreciated. In spite of that, he simply never felt that he fit into the new work situation in the same way that he had in the Boston scene where he had, in a very real sense, grown up within the company, where he knew his co-workers well and they knew him. This was hard on him.

By this time, only Claire and Debbie still lived at home. Over the years as each of the older members of the family moved out, the remaining girls gladly shifted around in the rooms upstairs. Finally it became possible for Art and Fran to move upstairs, converting their former bedroom into a comfortable family room. It opened up the whole downstairs and gave them a great place for watching television together and for entertaining company.

Claire, the family artist, noticed that, as yet, there was nothing at all on the wall behind the couch. She was taking woodworking classes in her art studies at that time. One evening, after several days and nights of buzzing noises, plus the distinctive smell of paint wafting upward from the cellar, Claire appeared in the room carrying a burnt orange colored creation. From a large piece of wood, she had adeptly designed a bright-petaled spring flower which she excitedly presented to her parents. Shortly thereafter, her flower was proudly hung on the wall above the couch.

Being grandparents delighted Art and Fran, stretching their personalities and lives in new directions. Their time and energy, even certain rooms in their home were readily adapted to their new role. They moved easily between parenting and grand-parenting, noting, of course that grandparents certainly had at least one noticeable advantage. They got to enjoy all the fun with the grandkids and then could hug and kiss them good-bye, handing them over to their parents as crankiness announced their nap, feeding or bedtime was near.

Art tried out the usual grandfather type names but was not satisfied with any of them. Grandpa, Gramps, or Papa did not really fit him yet, so there was a short period where he chose to be called ATD. Perhaps it had to do with that way he signed off on memos at work or as one story goes, it might have had to do with a raincoat incident at Filene's basement.

Filene's department store in Boston was famous for its price discounting system, whereby items were marked down on successive days following a definite pattern. Faithful customers from near and far came there for fantastic bargains. People were known to watch desired clothing items over a period of weeks before purchasing it at an incredible markdown. Art found a navy blue raincoat that he really liked. Having set his sights on it, he stopped in a few times to monitor the markdown process. Finally one day he went, ready to buy. He read the tag and realized that he had miscalculated and it was tomorrow, not today, that the discount would happen. Knowing that he could not return the next day, he asked Fran to go. She wanted to know how she would discover which one was "it", suspecting rightly that there was probably a whole rack to choose from. His blue eyes twinkled as he replied, "Just read the sales tags. You will have no doubt."

In she went, accompanied by Mary and Kelly. They began their detective work. Soon Fran found the area he described and the size he told her to look for. He had tucked his size 44 long in among the 32s for safe keeping. She called over to Mary and together they combed through the crowded rack, which actually had coats of several sizes all mixed together. Fran hadn't handled many price tags before her laughing could be heard down the aisle. She found ATD- ATD- ATD inscribed boldly again and again on both sides of the price tag. The cashier looked a bit askance at these scribbles but they didn't mind for they had succeeded. ATD had his new raincoat. The details of the story quickly spread through the family grapevine. The rest is history.

One other downtown store that he frequented whenever he needed a new hat was Raymond's, a large retail store that sold all kinds of clothing goods. It was prominently located in the heart of Boston's downtown shopping area and was especially famous for having counter after counter displaying men's hats. Hats were regular wear for men until John F. Kennedy became president in 1960. Kennedy seldom donned a hat. Within Kennedy's first year in office, the men of the country, in particular of Boston, began to imitate his hatless style. His generation moved on, leaving the regular custom of wearing hats behind them and leaving Raymond's in trouble.

As their children married and started their own homes, Art and Fran knew that relationships with them would also change in some ways. Their kids had a wife or husband now, were becoming parents and would have their own ways of parenting and of running a household. Art and Fran tried to support each one, helping out if they could or were asked. Otherwise they made every effort to just listen, be there but stay out of the way, keeping their own counsel, even biting their own tongue now and again.

They became creative at keeping in touch. Sometimes they burned up the phone lines or went over to visit a new apartment or house, offering to help paint, shop, cook or whatever might be needed. Before there were babies to watch, they often went bowling with some of their married children, maybe followed by lunch at Burger King. Another night they might cook a meal inviting some couple over or meeting them for an early bird special at a favorite restaurant. Invitations went both ways. They relished these maturing relationships with their kids and their spouses. Having the doorbell ring unexpectedly and someone just drop in at Hollingsworth Avenue for a surprise visit because they were in the neighborhood was a treat. Within minutes the teapot was on, more plates were out, food appeared and talk, laughter, perhaps even a hot game of cards might follow.

Art always loved cards, particularly Whist or Canasta. Many a new boyfriend met his Waterloo before the last hand of the game was over. As a typical game progressed, Art stayed involved in the flow of conversation yet somehow eyed every card, storing the information, knowing what each player still had in his or her hand. Often there then came that magical moment when, with a broad grin on his face, Art triumphantly dropped that winning card, absolutely sure of his victory. He was thrilled with himself.

Bowling was another favorite. On Saturdays at *Olindys* bowling was only twenty-five cents a string. Art and Fran often played several strings with Carol and John or others of their kids and their husbands. On their own, they had also been members of a co-ed bowling league for years. Fran was an excellent bowler, sometimes to Art's chagrin, topping his score royally. One evening Fran racked up a powerful total rivaling the highest male score of the night. The official score-keeper that night put Fran's name and score in the men's column, spelling it with the masculine form—Francis. It took a while for Art, and his male teammates, to live that one down.

Especially in the spring and fall, yard sales became part of their regular Saturday morning repertoire. Art scanned the local newspapers on Friday evening, working out a game plan for when and how to organize their yard sale route so they would get the most for their efforts. He learned the codes for what was on sale at each location: toys, clothing, furniture and more. This was a high tech effort. With a town map in hand, the stops were carefully plotted out. Some mornings they struck gold. Other Saturdays they had little luck, discovering only real duds. After a while they could simply drive by, assess possibilities and decide their moves accordingly. They became pros, passing on tips to anyone willing to listen. When they returned home they divided up the loot. Some things might be for themselves, others for one of the kids or grandkids. For years, the greatest number of purchases were tucked into hiding places upstairs until it was time to wrap them up for the annual Christmas "grab," a fun-filled family tradition celebrated during the pre-Christmas family gathering.

The years seemed to be flying by. Incredibly, retirement was coming onto the horizon as the late1970s approached. Art knew that his retirement check would be based on his earnings from the last three working years. He had been thinking along these lines around the time that an advancement opportunity arose within his own department at the Braintree office. He felt he was highly qualified for the position so he applied. He definitely had the background, years of service and the skills needed, but things were changing in the general work world and its influence was felt also at all levels within the halls of AT&T. Advanced educational degrees and computer savvy carried more and more weight in job resumes. A younger group of men called Junior Executives were being brought on board in many locations and groomed to move up the proverbial ladder. The older telephone company managers dubbed them the Jet Set.

In spite of this reality Art still felt confident, applied for the opening, asking his immediate supervisor for a recommendation. A few days later the report that his supervisor wrote accidentally crossed Arthur's desk. It was an excellent appraisal of Art's abilities, loyalty and experience. He definitely was described as a person who could handle the position well. The recommendation however ended briefly noting that Arthur T. Doyle was now a 63 year old employee, nearing retirement age.

Art neither got the position in the offing, nor did he receive an explanation of why not. After much thought and a consultation meeting with the Union representative Art filed a form for age discrimination, which he felt might be operating here. In those days there was not yet a critical mass in society nor within many major companies drawing attention to this particular issue regarding age in the workplace. In the end, from what he could ascertain, his filed complaint did not seem to receive much in-depth consideration. He shook his head sadly as he took this truth in, knowing that was the end of that hope. In spite of this difficult process, his last few years with the company passed quickly and well.

On June 29, 1978 at Lantana's Restaurant on the South Shore Art's family, friends and co-workers gathered to both toast and also roast him during his retirement party. One of the highlights of the evening was that his son sang a special solo tribute, *I Did It My Way*. Art Jr. adapted it to fit his Dad's life, re-naming it, *You Did It Your Way*. It was heartfelt and full of meaning, especially for the family members present. After forty plus years of service with the American Telephone and Telegraph Company, Art drank in each moment of a well deserved celebration.

On a clear crisp fall afternoon of 1978, Art gathered up his remaining belongings. He shook hands and exchanged greetings with each of his co-workers. Outside in the parking lot he piled his things onto the back seat of the car, turned the key in the ignition and headed the car toward the long curving driveway at the Mall, pointing his wheels toward Five Corners and the road home. He consciously took several deep breaths of the fresh brisk air, musing to himself about how quickly all those intervening years passed.

What would this new phase called retirement be like? What lay ahead for him, for them, was unclear, but somehow he felt that it would be okay. Besides, it only came one day at a time.

Living into Retirement

Art and Fran were in their mid-sixties, had good health and wore their ages well. For most of their adult lives their daily routine did not include being together, side by side all day in the same physical space. It was going to take some sort of re-negotiating to find their new rhythm.

They still had two children living at home, but they knew that was not for long. Deb, the youngest, was almost 21, studying at Catherine Laboure School of Nursing in Dorchester and dating her high school boyfriend, George Soligan. Claire had finished college, was looking for a job as an art teacher, and contemplating a move down toward the Cape Cod area.

While working at Falmouth High School, Claire met Kevin Cavanaugh, her future husband, who served in the US Coast Guard. Art played a small but important role in Claire's movement toward a final decision. Claire, a tall attractive blonde, had had several suitors over the years, but admitted one day that she somehow was expecting to know clearly, within herself, when Mr. Right came along, something like seeing stars or hearing bells. A year or more after she began dating Kevin, whom the family liked, dubbing him Kevin from heaven, Art spontaneously decided one evening to see if he could help this cause along. As Claire and Kevin were together on the front porch kissing one another good night, Art grabbed two bells from a nearby shelf in the television room, leaned out the window and rang them for all he was worth. Claire heard the sound, got the message and cracked up laughing.

After a month or so of their newly established retirement routine, Fran knew clearly that decision time had come. Having Art at her heels all day was not going to work for her. Of this, she now had no doubts whatever. Perhaps they could divide things up. Fran could care for all that went on inside the house, barring repairs. Art could organize maintenance, plus everything outside the house: the yard, the garage and more. Fran encouraged him to get to those home improvements that, for years now, had been put aside for some rainy day. Art enjoyed getting engrossed in projects and she was going to be his best cheerleader.

Since Art had ordinarily done the weekly food shopping, he considered that an outside activity, so that was a keeper. In former years he made sketchy attempts at scanning newspapers and flyers for coupons to stretch the family budget. Now, with time on his side, this truly became a work of art. He knew the setup of every local grocery store, knew what the family liked to eat, and so he began to approach the weekly shopping expedition with all his native organizational fervor. At that same time he made a choice that from then on he would commit some money each week to purchasing non-perishables for the Vincent de Paul food bank at church.

Every weekend he cut, sorted and lined up the coupons, (single, double and even triples) by aisles, calculating how to get the most for his money. Eventually his pursuit became contagious to the cashiers at the local Stop and Shop. They aided and abetted the weekly adventure of seeing what part of the bill could be paid with coupons. He proudly preserved one grocery receipt from Shaw's where he paid for 98% of the cost of the groceries with his coupons alone. It was his red letter day.

Right up until Art was around 93 he looked forward to the newspaper's arrival so he could study the bargains. By then, he was no longer able to buzz up and down the aisles of the local grocery store, but from his command chair at home he could enlist everyone around to do his shopping with him or for him. For a time, he got his Hospice workers to drive him to the local store for these weekly purchases. Finally he decided to let go of actively shopping and just increase his Sunday offering a bit. After that, week after week as he entered the side door of Kateri Tekakwitha Church, he checked out the food barrel near the entrance. If he found it empty he lamented not having bags of groceries to deposit there himself.

One day early on in his retirement, while scanning the *Boston Globe,* Art caught sight of an advertisement from H & R Block for seniors willing to learn the ins and outs of doing taxes for the elderly. He signed up, took the courses in Tax Counseling for the Elderly and passed the exam with no trouble. He set up shop a few days a week at the Braintree Senior Citizen Center only a short drive from home. Tax return deadlines were fast approaching. He was ready to make a go of it.

He was intrigued by the level of listening involved with each client. He experienced a strong interpersonal, almost pastoral aspect to many interviews. This was unexpected, yet he slipped into it so naturally that anyone would have thought he had training. As men or women sat down with tax forms, sales slips, invoices and former returns, they also carried with them their own personal lives. He listened attentively to the story of how the past year had unfolded, the human conditions behind the numbers. Some had lost a spouse, suffered a heart attack, closed up a home full of memories and moved in with a daughter or a son. Many, especially older women, came timidly, feeling quite vulnerable, even lost, never having needed to be the one doing this tax business before. For more than a dozen years Art came back each year, received their stories and helped as much as he could. In some cases where needs were evident, he might refer someone to a local agency or practically complete the requisite forms for them. Beyond the forms, he might promise a prayer that their concerns be resolved in a positive way. People returned year after year.

There were times when Art, Fran and sometimes Fran's sister, Mary, who lived nearby, joined the field trips offered through the Senior Center. Whenever Art spoke about his involvement there he spoke about helping them with their taxes, giving the distinct impression that, despite his advancing years, he did not yet see himself as one of the elderly.

Eventually, Art's tax skills were noticed by the H&R group with whom he worked. They invited him to work at one of their larger centers within Sears & Roebucks Company at the Braintree Mall. After just a few weeks there, he knew that doing taxes with younger folk crossed some line for him. The complications of separations, divorces, two households with young kids split between husband and wife for x number of weeks or months of the year were just more intricate and involved than his mind and heart wanted to be at this moment in his life. He persevered for a season or two, learning many of the intricacies of such tax forms. With all he learned, he was able to help some of his own grown kids with filing their returns for several years to come. The Internal Revenue Service, the Tax Counseling Committee for the Elderly and H&R Block each, at different periods during these years, awarded Art with certificates of recognition and appreciation for his faithful, dedicated service.

For years in Braintree, Art and Fran's closest friends were two couples, Dottie and Mary, who were blood sisters and their husbands, Eddie and Jimmy. Fran, Mary and Dottie were probably the best shoppers in town, at least the most devoted. Just let them get a whiff of a great sale within a thirty mile radius and they had their coats on and handbags ready for travel. They captured Debbie as she came out of school, tucked her in the car with them and off they went in search of treasures. The three families celebrated birthdays, anniversaries and graduations together, plus all the smaller but significant moments in between. Their everyday lives were woven together through thick and thin. Mutual support could be counted on whenever, wherever, however needed.

As the decades passed, life circumstances in each family began to shift. Mary's children married and headed out to the warmth and sunshine of the west coast. She missed them terribly, especially because she was not near her young grandchildren while they were growing up. Soon she and Jimmy bit the bullet and were California bound. A few years later, when Eddie reached retirement age, he left his job at the *Boston Globe,* deciding that he had shoveled enough snow, endured enough of New England's cold weather. He and Dottie began entertaining the prospect of life in the snowless, warmer reality of California. What they at first just entertained, soon began to take shape.

During what began as a casual conversation one night on the back porch at Hollingsworth Avenue, a travel plan was hatched. It hinged on the agreement that if this car trip out to California could be transformed into a tour of the country, Art and Fran would join Dottie and Eddie in driving out and then they would fly back. There were so many places all four of them had always wanted to see, so why not make a real adventure out of this cross country move? They must have had a great conversation that evening because within the next three weeks they packed their bags, told their families, gassed up the car, pulled out the maps and headed west.

Eddie wanted to visit a fellow war veteran, so the first stop was New York City; then on to the Liberty Bell in Philly;

further south to the battlefields of Gettysburg...and so it went. They wanted to drink it all in. They were having the time of their lives. Art and Fran's kids called one another frequently to see if anyone knew exactly where the folks were. Sometimes it was “Yes, they are as far as...” There were other nights when no one had a clue. With no cell phones or computers available to demand instant contact, their adult children back home had to be content with phone calls now and again. They would joke with one another asking, “Do we know where our parents are tonight?”

The travelers stopped when the spirit or some scenic attraction moved them. They were especially taken by the natural beauty surrounding them; the open plains, gorgeous mountains, the marvels of the Grand Canyon. They mutually decided that they could not pass up a detour to Las Vegas. Once they arrived and booked into a hotel, Art went to find a phone to call one of the kids. When he did not return to the room after a half hour, Fran got worried and went looking for him. She was sure something was wrong back east and he was trying to figure out how to tell her. Instead when she reached the main Casino entrance, she caught a glimpse of him in the distance, and heard his laugh across the room above the din of the machines. He had tossed a few coins into a slot machine as he made his way across the floor to the lineup of phones against a back wall. All of a sudden bells and whistles sounded and quarters began pouring out. Art scooped them into his bulging pants pockets as fast as he could, loving every minute of it. Dinner was on him that night.

Once they reached the west coast, they explored Dottie and Eddie's new surroundings: Nine mile drive, Golden Gate Bridge, Alcatraz and more. One night, after a full day of touring, they trudged back to the car dog tired, ready to head to the house, only to realize that the key was IN the car with all doors securely locked. It was already 9:00 p.m. They knew they would pay a pretty penny to get a locksmith at this time of night, but consideration of the price of hotel rooms made the call to a local shop easier to do. Luck was with them. A kind obliging locksmith replied in the affirmative and relatively quickly came to their rescue with all the tools of his trade. From that day onward, there was always an extra car key securely taped onto the inside flap of Art's wallet.

On a steel grey, rain soaked morning, the ride to the airport and the tough good-byes began. Braintree was going to be a lonelier place without Dottie, Eddie, Mary, Jimmy and the kids. They had been like local uncles and aunts to the Doyle kids. They could not be replaced. Although they found ways to keep in touch over the years, the three couples were never again all together in one place.

Back on home turf again, with no more trips on the horizon, Art took a serious look at the house, deciding that major repairs were needed to the roof of the house and the garage. Replacing the damaged shingles would be an expensive proposition. After some calculating, he figured that he might both speed up the work and save money if he did some of the preliminary work himself. He had the time and felt it was within his scope to remove the garage shingles. He bought the scaffolding and supplies from the local Home Depot. Read all the intricate instructions. He was ready.

One mild fall morning he strode into the back yard straight from the breakfast table, full of energy and determination. Painstakingly he checked and secured the scaffolding, gathered his tools and climbed into working position. Things proceeded well along the whole right side of the garage. With each passing day, as another section was completed, Art's confidence grew. Piles of loosened shingles littered the ground, needing to be piled up each evening. Toward the end of the third day he was reaching the front end of the garage, moving the scaffolding carefully as he inched along.

He was hot, tired and glad to see the day's end in view. There were just a few more shingles close to the edge. He would finish those, then quit. As he stretched across to unhinge one of them, he felt a chill race through his body. The scaffolding made a slight but undeniable shift beneath him. Before he could re-balance or grab anything for support, the scaffolding swayed further. He lost his footing, lurched backwards and fell to the ground with a thud.

Stunned and covered with dust, he checked for broken bones. With the sharp ache he was feeling he was surprised not to discover any. He sat on the ground as pain pulsated through different parts of his body. Eventually, it subsided enough that Art could breathe normally and he decided it was time to move into the house. With slow steps he winced his way onto the back porch and into the kitchen. There he found Fran and

Debbie chatting at the kitchen table. Stunned by his appearance, they strongly suggested going directly to the local emergency room. He would hear none of it. He wanted to go upstairs into his own bed, protesting that he would feel better in the morning. Art also insisted that Deb take her mother to Bingo at Sacred Heart Parish Hall that evening as planned. Fran's sister, Mary would be expecting them. What he needed was rest. They watched protectively as he made his way upstairs before they left the house by way of the backyard, where the scaffolding lay in mangled disarray against the side of the garage.

Once Art hit the second floor he searched the bathroom closet for Epsom Salt, filled the tub with warm water, edged his way in and sank into its soothing relief. He left the tub only when the waters became too cool for comforting. Debbie called the house a few times that evening, trying to reassure herself that he was okay, but Art was not leaving his warm sudsy cocoon for any phone call. Once he felt better, he eased himself onto his bed, sinking into a deep exhausted sleep. About an hour later he woke sore all down one side. This pattern repeated itself off and on during the night.

By morning he was miserable enough to head to the South Shore Hospital Emergency Room where a cursory examination failed to show anything more dramatic than bruising, scratches and soreness. Armed with a prescription for pain meds and advice to stay off the heights, he was sent home.

A second trip to the same ER the following day, even with additional symptoms, brought neither satisfactory answers nor serious concern from medical personnel. Art was sure that this diagnosis was wrong. Debbie insisted that they head to Carney Hospital in Dorchester, where she trained as an R.N, knew doctors and felt sure he would get the help he obviously needed. Art offered no resistance whatsoever. She said to her mother "Grab a toothbrush, razor and whatever. We're on our way."

Within hours of their arrival at the hospital, Art was placed on an IV. He smiled, knowing that now they would not send him home. He was admitted over the Columbus Day weekend and was monitored carefully. Through a series of tests a diagnosis slowly emerged. X-rays showed thick dark blood clots in his abdominal and leg areas, any one of which could loosen and travel to his heart in an instant. Doctors were unsure whether his body could or would absorb them. They did not know what lay beneath them, since the x-rays could not penetrate.

His condition worsened as the days passed. He had received several units of blood; had one leg that was painfully swollen; the shadow on his kidney was growing larger; while his kidney function levels deteriorated. The medical team began advising Fran that Art's condition was unstable and quite serious.

Finally, came the day when the head surgeon felt a decision had to be made... and now. It was time to operate. There was no time to call in another specialist and go through the process of getting a second opinion. Not to remove the clots had become as risky as any operation might be. At least surgery, IF successful, gave him a better chance of recovery and of having a normal life again. Fran was with Deb when the doctor laid it all out. She almost passed out, and Deb, who was then eight months pregnant, likewise. Unflappably the Dr. completed his information. His closing statement being, “We don’t deliver babies here.”

Now he needed Art’s consent to do the surgery, risks and all. Dr. Ferrante, Art’s primary physician for many years, was called in. He and Deb talked with Art, who in his present condition could not take in even the mini-version of the facts that they were offering. He cut to the chase, asking them directly if this had to be done. When told “Yes, it did.” he gave consent.

The night before surgery Art was heavily sedated. Fran was beside Art’s bed when the doctor came in to check him out before finishing his rounds. She assured him that she, the whole family and friends would be praying for him each moment during the operation. He thanked her and left for the evening.

Fran did not want to leave the hospital room that evening, but since Art was in a four bed unit, staying was out of the question by hospital regulations. She stood by his bed pouring out her heart to him, never knowing if he heard even a word. She could not be at peace with this kind of a good-bye. What if it were her last?

When her kids were ready to drive Fran home, she was nowhere to be found, not in the visitor's area, nor the restroom, nor the corridor. Where could she be? A soft knocking came from Art's walk-in locker in the corner of the room, Fran's voice accompanying the sound. " Let me out." They laughed in spite of the seriousness of everything. What was she doing in there? She wasn't thinking clearly but knew she couldn't leave without a real "good-bye." A hospital call to Dr. Ferrante brought an assurance that if Fran got to the hospital before 6:30 a.m. the following morning, he would see that she got to speak to him. Trusting him, she agreed to leave.

The following day, true to his word, Dr. Ferrante was there when the stretcher arrived to take Art upstairs. He told the attendants they could not go anywhere until Art's wife arrived. Within minutes, Claire and Fran came off the elevator and headed right over to the waiting stretcher. She leaned over, spoke tenderly, kissed him on the forehead, then, she could let him go.

In one sense, from that moment on, time stood still. In reality, they did not have to wait long for the surgery to be over, about an hour. The doctor walked into the waiting room and sat down with Fran. He said he believed that they had gotten all the clots and stemmed the bleeding. The damage had been much more extensive than the pre-op tests had revealed because the density of the blood clots concealed the severity of what was underneath. With time, care, and prayers, he was convinced Art had a fine chance of getting better. He cautioned that the full healing process would be slow and arduous. Fran grasped his hands in gratitude and utter relief.

It was touch and go for the first days, but in due time, Art recovered, moved into rehab and began trying to walk again. He weighed less than 150 pounds, had lost muscle tone and body strength. It was going to take hard work to get back in physical shape again. Because of his condition he had to wear special support stockings for a few months. He complained loudly about the bother of pulling them off and on each day, until his wife and daughters calmly informed him that this kind of thing was an everyday ritual for them. He would have to look elsewhere for sympathy.

Art improved a little more each week. Eventually, it was time for him to be released from rehab.

On a bitter cold November day, they wheeled him to the enclosed front entrance of the hospital. Although he looked frail, he felt like one lucky man that morning. Once outside the doors of the building, wrapped tightly in two colorful hand-made afghans, he took in long deep breaths of the fresh air. Roughly six weeks after the accident, he was alive, could walk a bit, was on the road to recovery and going home with Fran, and his family. He would be there for the Thanksgiving celebration with lots to be grateful for. His doctors told him to get right back into living, doing each day what his strength and common sense dictated. He couldn't wait to begin.

Interestingly, as he labored shakily to ascend the front steps of the house on Hollingsworth Avenue, with his daughters supporting him on each side and Fran bringing up the rear, he never once thought to pause, even for one moment, to notice the fine new roof on the house or on the garage out back.

Art's Dad - James Patrick Doyle: m-1910

1873-C. Sligo, Ireland : 1946-Boston,MA

James, son George, wife Catherine (Connell)

Catherine: 1879 C. Sligo, Ireland-1978 Boston, MA

Anne (McDermott) - Peter Keane - m 1911

Anne- 1889 C. Roscommon, Ireland : 1936 Boston, MA
Peter- 1888 C. Galway, Ireland : 1915 Boston, MA

Older brother Jimmy and Art - c. 1916

Fran's older sister Mary and Fran - c. 1917

Retouched photo Art presented at Jimmy's 70th birthday

Art's "new car"

Art, Fran, and Art Jr - 1936

Art and a younger brother, George, Mission Hill

Art Jr. and Sr. at Nana and Papa's house-Hillside St, Roxbury

Siblings: Jimmy, Paul, Anne, Art, Helen, George (Paul's twin, Frank, drowned in 1956.)

Back row: Joan, Art Jr. Art Sr, Barb

Front: Nancy, Mary, Carol in Art's arms

679 Parker St - 1949

Paul and Mary Doyle's wedding 1950

Art- behind and to the right of Paul
Fran- front row- black/white hat.

Fran and Art at Monti's party.
She's not thrilled to be photographed

First house they owned. 65 Hillside St, Roxbury

Art Relaxing in his Braintree Home

Joan's 25th Jubilee - 1983: Art, Arthur, Carol, Claire

Front: Barbie, Joan, Mary, Nancy, and Deb

Claire and Kevin's wedding - Sept 6, 1989 - Carol, Joan, Arthur, Mary, Kevin, Claire, Art, Barb, Debbie, Nancy

Kaitlyn, Tami and Fred discovered the kitchen candy closet

Mary and David's daughter, Kelly: died Sept 16, 1993

Doesn't seem that Shevonne or

Michael got Art's musical talent

Sons-in-laws at 65th wedding anniversary - 2000

Jimmy Connor (Nancy), Dick Nolan (Barb), John Nickerson (Carol), Art and Fran, George Soligan (Deb), David Chaves (Mary), Kevin Cavanaugh (Claire)

4th of July, Frans's birthday

Carol, Claire, Deb, Barbie, Nancy, Joanie - Beverly Manor Nursing Home

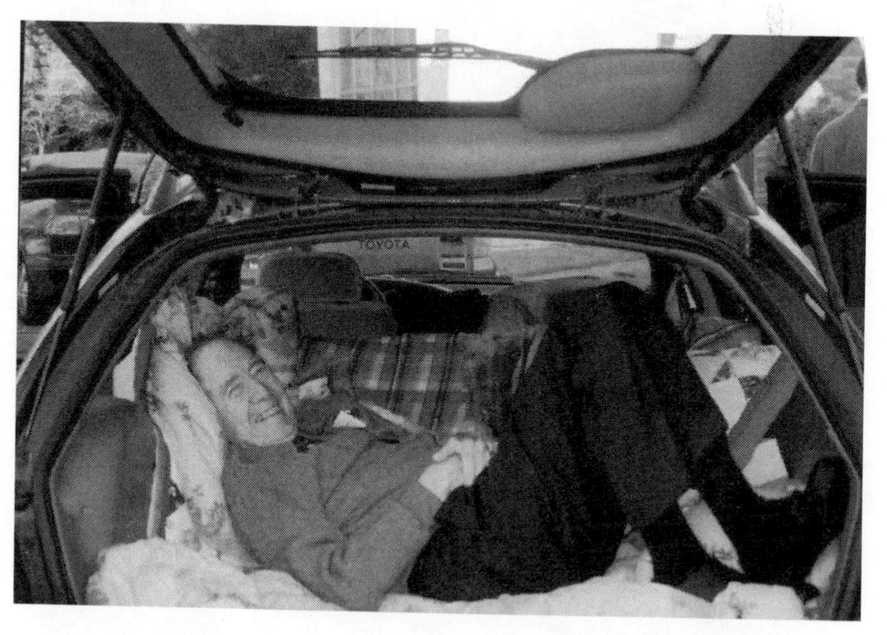

Art's "luxury" accommodations to Foxwoods

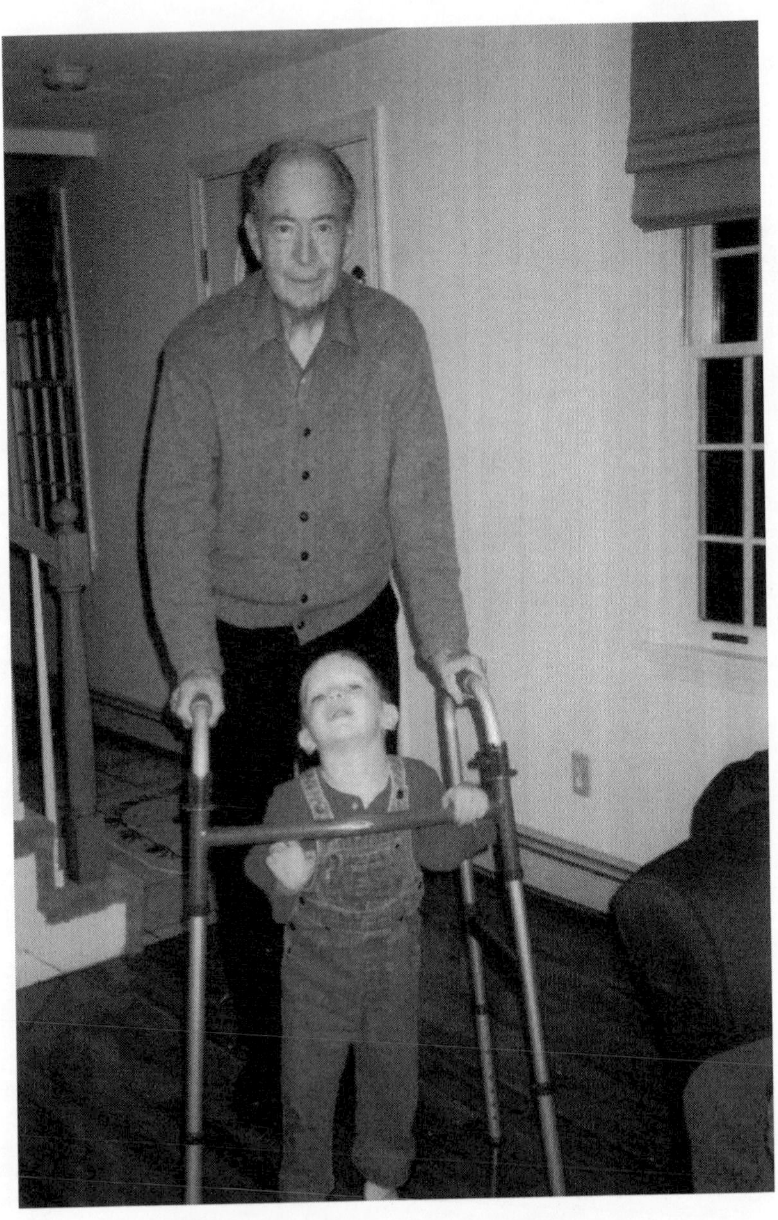

C'mon, let's run now - Art and Owen

A quiet reflective moment - c. 2007

Five Generations: Art, his son Arthur (top right), grandson Danny (top left), two great granddaughters Alicia and Lindsay, Lindsay's daughter Paige

Birthday gift for Art's 90th

Art , his son-in-law Dick and the pilot

Scratch tickets - YEAH! Winnings ???

(Jimmy and Art)

John Jepson and Art at Saturday evening Liturgy, Kateri, Tekakwitha Church, Plymouth

Eighty and Beyond

As years moved along, so did the inevitable process of aging. Off and on Art noticed disturbing changes in Fran, days when she was quite pale, had visible tremors, even what seemed to be momentary blackouts. They talked together and with their three daughters who were nurses, Barb, Mary and Deb. They then made an appointment with Dr. Ferrante at Carney Hospital. An array of tests revealed that Fran was suffering from an unpredictable form of brain seizures for which there was no known cure and no real certainty about a course of treatment. Different medications like Dilantin or Tegretol might help, but then again with some patients they did not. In the long run, the message was that whatever was used could not be guaranteed to eliminate nor fully control these recurring episodes.

At first the incidents came almost imperceptibly, ending almost as quickly as they appeared. As time passed, they progressed steadily. Each seizure lasted just that tiny bit longer, its after effects undeniable. Some attacks sent Fran crashing to the floor without warning. Art felt totally at a loss when these occurred. More than once he resorted to 911 for immediate assistance. At first the paramedics took Fran right to the emergency room, but sometimes, by the time they arrived, she had come out of the episode, had good blood pressure readings and was sitting up wondering how she got to the ER and not at all happy to be there. Over time, as everyone became more familiar with her symptoms, a list of things to try before calling 911was put into practice. This did little to lessen Art's fears and in no way cut down the number of times symptoms re-occurred. At least there was, for Fran, the small consolation that the piercing sound of police car sirens plus the appearance of a fire truck and ambulance outside the Hollingsworth Ave address became more rare.

Gradually Fran's doctor advised limitations on her activities. Ordinary daily events like walking down the stairs, going out into the street alone or cooking over the stove became potentially risky moments. Art adapted his lifestyle, helping Fran with whatever she needed. He put his hand to hair dressing becoming somewhat adept at cutting, dyeing and even attempting to style Fran's hair. He learned the art of painting her nails for special occasions. Everyday household tasks were part of his new repertoire. He took over the kitchen, cultivating a few more culinary skills, enough to produce a hot, relatively nutritious evening meal. Thank God, the Doyle daughters initiated an effective "meals on wheels" program to broaden the choices, sometimes offering to re-do Fran's hair while they were there.

In the early years of the seizures, months could pass between incidents. Art and Fran kept life as normal as possible. They hoped that each period of no attacks meant that the medication was kicking in. Each recurrence proved them depressingly wrong. They picked themselves up as best they could and moved on. Life still had lots to offer. They were determined to live it as fully as possible.

The grandchildren were growing. There were school photos to frame, sports events, plays, recitals, Grandparents' days to attend. Art and Fran went as often as they could. They made sure there were kid treats around the house. A cupboard above the clothes dryer was a well-stocked candy closet. Desserts were easy to find. The bottom drawer in the TV room bulged with toys for kids of all ages. Games abounded both in house and in the garage. The house was thoroughly child-proofed for safety, but child-friendly in all other ways. None of this was lost on the young ones, who loved to visit this mini-Toys-R-US.

Some, to the chagrin of their parents, arrived, just about kissed their grandparents, pulled a chair over to the candy closet or pulled open the toy drawer. Others just ran through the kitchen, blew a kiss as they headed right out to the back yard to play. It might be an hour or more before they were heard from again, their parents checking on them from the screened-in porch where nothing could be missed. At times everyone eventually joined them outside, relishing the fun.

In the back yard with its slanted driveway, perched at different levels on the side of the garage Art, the former basketball player and referee, set up three basketball hoops with balls that fit each one. The lowest rung was for the pint-sized kids. They just "put" the ball through the net, grinning and squealing with delight as their parents applauded. The middle basket required a bit of height, moderate throwing skills plus some idea of the game. The regulation-sized hoop was hung properly, at the official height, near the top of the garage door, offering a real sports challenge. Art's idea,

"Let everyone be Larry Byrd for a day."

How each grandson (some granddaughters too) loved to engage with their grandfather at that basket. Even in his later years, Art could often beat his grandsons or great-grandsons at a game of 21, which required accuracy of the throw, not speed or range of movement. Once, Art Jr's teen-aged grandson, Corey, was visiting from Oklahoma. His dad, Bryan, had taken on his grandfather in the past, winning some and losing others. When Corey decided he wanted to shoot a few hoops, Bryan found himself a good seat to watch the match. Bryan smiled as the score started out swaying back and forth, but before very long the points began mounting in Art's favor. Finally, as Art's last throw slid smoothly through the hoop, someone yelled "twenty-one." He had won. The game was finished and for the moment so was Corey, who found it hard to believe what had just happened to him. His great-grandfather might be old, but he was good.

Into the midst of this enjoyment of their children, grandchildren and great-grandchildren a thunderbolt struck in September of 1993. Barb and Dick were shaken from their sleep by a phone call from Debbie in the early hours of the morning of the seventeenth. There was no sleeping after the conversation. They waited until after the heavier morning rush hour traffic before they got into their car and headed north to Braintree, arriving in less time than expected, which for once, did not please them. They had not spoken much during the half hour drive. There was little to say.

When Barb got to the top step of Art and Fran's house and reached for the handle of the outer door, she paused for a moment. Whispering another prayer, she rang the bell. Then, she and Dick walked inside, crossed the living room and greeted her parents who were reclining in their chairs reading the morning paper, half listening to the television in the background. Fran immediately sensed something, noticing how pale Barb looked. Instinctively, she sat up in her chair and switched off the television, leaving a sudden silence hanging in the room. Barb and Dick lowered themselves onto the sofa, sitting shoulder to shoulder. Barb had prepared what she would say before leaving Plymouth, but now facing Art and Fran in person, Barb's voice faltered. Haltingly, she began sharing the news that Mary and David's only child, their nineteen-year-old daughter, Kelly, had died last evening in Little Compton, Rhode Island. It had been raining. Her car had somehow gone over the edge of a pier, plunging into the deep black waters below. Neither the emergency crew nor the hospital personnel had been able to save her.

"Oh God, no! no!" Art covered his eyes with both hands. Fran sat straight, rigid, almost frozen in place. She stared intently at her daughter, obviously unable to fully grasp what was being said. Not a word passed her lips. Barb moved further out on the cushion, her hands resting on her mother's knees.

She spoke again forming her words slowly and carefully, trying to add the few known details that might help her mother take in something of this horrific news. “Not our Kelly,” Fran stammered. Her voice carried a last ditch hope that she was not hearing correctly. Almost in a whisper, Barb nodded her head and said, “Yes, Mom, our Kelly.”

The truth was excruciatingly painful, gripping them, sucking them into an empty blackness. “God, oh my God, how can this be?” Fran sobbed. Their granddaughter, Kelly, who had lived with them for more than a year in the mid-seventies, while her Dad, David, was in the Air Force in Iran. Kelly, who learned to walk in this room, who spoke her first words in this very house, who danced in her playpen to John Denver’s hit songs. Kelly was dead? Art held Fran, their minds and bodies numb, their hearts breaking.

In a flash of terrible realization, they asked almost in chorus, “What about Mary and David? We have to call them, but... ” They were speechless. Their own beings still rejecting the full impact as too awful to be true. They would gladly give their own lives to bring Kelly back. They knew the raw truth that such exchanges cannot be.

Somehow, they moved through the days of the wake and funeral, drawing on deep resources of faith, being lovingly present to and with their daughter, son-in-law, and the whole family. Kelly was now home with God, gone far, far too soon, absolutely, but at least safe in God.

After the funeral services at church, the long line of cars wended its way through the town turning left into the Middletown Cemetery, just outside the town of Portsmouth. The cars came to a stop at the gravesite near the back of the cemetery, in a broad open area. Family members drew in close, then closer, holding one another in grief. Many of Kelly's high school classmates and friends were there clutching flowers, tears streaking their young faces. After the local priest offered brief burial prayers, Art moved forward slightly to read an Irish Blessing. His voice sounded strained as he spoke the first line. His tall frame bent forward, shoulders heaved just slightly. Those near him edged in closer, pressing supportive hands against his back, joining their sorrow- laden voices with his, until they completed the final line.

The effect of this sudden loss was profound and far-reaching. Good-byes could never quite be the same again. An awareness life's fragility, the finality of death and the irreplaceable preciousness of each person sank into the bedrock of what might be called the common family heart, a profound sorrow shared.

Weeks and months passed. It seemed incredible that the demands of ordinary living would not stop for a while to allow time for grieving. But life has that inexorable way of moving along, demanding that attention be given to outward events even as one continues to carry the heavy weight of grief.

One of several outward things for Art was beginning to do some long-range planning for himself and Fran. As they hit three score plus ten and counting, he continued reading and researching long-term health care possibilities, in case either of them would one day need to be placed in a nursing home. Massachusetts' Insurance Law # 211, CMR 65,000 focused on that issue. He read and re-read it carefully. The law, as it was written, both intrigued and irked him. It intrigued him because it stated that if you bought this long-term care insurance and later entered a nursing facility you could be guaranteed that no future financial recovery would be made from your estate. This seemed a great security to have. It allowed the older citizen to be assured that the home they cherished and the savings they put aside as an inheritance for their children would actually go to them and not eventually into the state coffers. As Art mulled this over, he did the math on how the State had calculated the finances of this insurance. What irked him was that he could not see why the individual citizen could not do this same thing and not have to give the specified amount of money to the government at all. He studied the law diligently, researched other states, calculated and came up with an alternative proposal that would allow a senior citizen to fulfill the same financial requirements of the state law, but do it by depositing the exact required amount of money in his or her own account, thereby becoming "self-insured" for long-term care.

He sent copies of his proposal to many state and some national politicians and to groups like AARP. He wrote articles for local newspapers and senior citizen circulations.

The response was mixed. Some never replied; while others acknowledged receiving it, letting the proposal die there. A few contacted him for more information, which he supplied eagerly. A Senator in Massachusetts asked Art to come in person to address the Congressional Health Commission presenting his findings and answering questions that might arise.

The woman on deck before him that evening had a proposal regarding breast cancer research which caught the media's eye, so eager local TV crews were on hand. As they spanned the chamber, their cameras caught glimpses of Art. He looked impressive in shirt, tie and suit, sitting in the row of upcoming speakers, flanked by his son-in-law, Dick, and his granddaughter, Joan. He did get to speak making a passionate presentation and answering several questions, but left unsure if he had really been heard and understood. When all was said and done, his proposal, although initially well received, died somewhere in congressional committee work. Where? Art never knew for he received no further communication from anyone at the statehouse. Even in his last years he sometimes wondered why this plan could not have worked and worked out well for many senior citizens.

As part of Art's daily routine, he went for a doctor-recommended walk each afternoon up and down the local streets, in order to stay healthy and limber. So it was not unusual one cold December day in 1997 for him to head out on a quick afternoon walk to and from the corner mail box, one block away. While he was gone, Fran got up to do something, caught her heel on the living room rug and fell forward with a bang. Art was devastated when he came in, the day's mail in hand, and found her on the floor moaning softly. Immediately, he called an ambulance and one of his kids. Fran was rushed to Carney Hospital; her right hip was broken and needed immediate replacement. The surgery went well, although it greatly disorientated her initially. For her recovery work it was decided to send her to Braintree Rehab near home, plus it was where Jeri, their grandson Jim's fiancée, was a physical therapist.

The rehab process proved quite difficult. Fran was a good patient, willing to work hard to get back as much mobility as possible. She came to each session with energy and determination, but try as she would, the accumulation of so many mini-seizures over the years had taken a toll. Fran could not remember the fine points of the therapist's instructions from one day to the next. Therefore, she was not getting in or out of her chair correctly, nor doing the practice exercises in her room according to the pattern taught. Gradually, her care plan pointed toward releasing her from rehab. Fran was recovering some mobility but definitely not enough to walk independently. She was even a bit unsteady when she tried moving with her walker.

She would need more assistance with her everyday activities than Art could give her by himself. With that news in hand, everyone went home to ponder "What next?" Realistically, it was clear that Art and Fran could not go back home by themselves, even on a trial basis. Concretely that meant they had to be moved and moved soon.

No one will ever really know what it cost Art those next few days to help pack up Fran and himself, to leave their home after more than 40 years of life there. They loved that barnyard red house on Hollingsworth Avenue. It was filled with wonderful family memories. Yet, Art accepted that Fran needed more care, so if this was the way to get it, then this was the best for him too. He also knew full well how fortunate he was to have a place to go on such short notice. They left Hollingsworth Avenue that very week.

Meanwhile, over in Medfield, Debbie's household and their lives were also undergoing radical changes, ones that cost, but would allow her family to welcome Art and Fran into their home. Ever since her high school years, Debbie had dated George Soligan from Braintree. When George graduated from law school, they married and settled in the town of Medfield. By now they had three kids, ages eight to thirteen.

After surveying the space in their home and considering their lives, the Soligans decided that with some give and take they could make a bedroom, a small bathroom and a living room space available. Even a small refrigerator could be installed for storing treats. Deb wanted them to be a part of her family scene and yet tried to create space in which they would have as much privacy and independence as they could handle. Little did she know that soon and very soon her living room would become Art's new "command central."

Art and Fran arrived with the belongings they thought they would need, not expecting to be there for a really long time. Once they settled in, Deb began doing exercises with her mother each day to see how much strength Fran might regain, especially in terms of walking. Daily attention and coaching brought noticeable improvement, but not enough to make returning to their home in Braintree an option.

For about four and a half years Art and Fran relished being adoring grandparents and forming special bonds with Kaitlyn, Tami, Fred and lots of their friends. On the evening of Kaitlyn's junior prom she spontaneously wrapped her arms around her grandmother's shoulders including her in a photo being taken with her prom date. Kaitlyn did not realize that with that simple gesture she was making history, actually opening up an opportunity that had not been there for decades. Fran had not had her picture taken for roughly fifty years or more. If anyone snuck a photo of her at an event, she somehow had a knack for finding out and the picture vanished. There was not even a photo of Art and Fran from the day of their wedding. This snapshot was a real breakthrough. For Fran's part she could no longer remember why she had not wanted to have her picture taken for so many years. She wondered about it, even out loud. No one who knew the 'why' offered to fill in the story. From then on, having your picture taken with Fran became a special treat.

By the summer of 2001, the demographics of Medfield had grown to the point where the town planners decided to make major improvements in their sewerage system. The summer months were targeted for the work so as not to interrupt the regular school schedule. By late spring teams of workers began digging up streets and laying pipes in earnest. This meant that moving into the summer months the water supply would be erratic at best which was not a great scenario for such a full household on Ledgetree Road in Medfield.

The Doyle girls talked back and forth and then talked some more. Who was able to help out for the summer months? Barb and Dick offered to have Art and Fran move in with them during the change-over. Only recently they had expanded the size of their mobile home quite a bit and felt they could accommodate them. Art and Fran packed their belongings again and headed south to the Plymouth Mobile Estates.

It was a wonderful summer. Plymouth is a tourist town located directly on the water. The protected harbor has a local marina where yachts of all descriptions move in and out with ease and beauty. With Plymouth Rock, the replica of the Mayflower, the Plymouth Plantation, stretches of sandy beach front, restaurants galore and ice cream stands, it was a great place to live through the summer months.

With a small church named Blessed Kateri Tekakwitha near the house, safe streets for Art to get his exercise each day, and adequate room within the house, life was good. Art and Fran could drive down to the harbor, watch the visitors in town and partake of whatever struck their fancy. Saturday evenings after Mass, they would pick up a meal at the Lobster Hut, park near the water's edge and simply enjoy the ocean breeze together. Like everyone else in town, they learned to protect their food from the seagulls emboldened by years of successfully swooping down and robbing meals from unsuspecting tourists.

During the years Art was there, the Lobster Hut became one of his favorite eating spots. For one of his birthdays, his kids were trying to upscale him to a nicer restaurant. With a confident twinkle in his eyes, he declared to anyone who would listen that they were free to eat the noon meal wherever they liked on August 11th, but if they wanted to celebrate his birthday with him, he would be at the Lobster Hut for lunch!

Living in Plymouth, they were also closer to more of their daughters, Barbie, Nancy and Carol; to granddaughters Elicia, Jean and Jody, grandsons Jimmy and his wife Jeri, plus Michael; and some of the great grandchildren too: Joey, John, Owen. The summer months moved along quickly, but unfortunately the sewerage project in Medfield did not do likewise. As often happens with town funded work, the projected deadlines came and went. Worse still, no one could say for sure when the final stage would be completed. So, Art and Fran happily stayed on in Plymouth as the new school year began.

Multi-colored leaves began piling up at the edges of the yard around Barb and Dick's house. Days were shorter, a coolness settling in toward evening. Fall crispness was in the air. On an otherwise ordinary afternoon in the beginning of October, Art and Fran sat chatting with their daughter, Mary, who had come up from Rhode Island for a visit. Barb was preparing something in the kitchen. They were all talking back and forth while half-watching the TV, when suddenly Fran became agitated. She seemed to be struggling with her breathing, to be experiencing sharp quick pains. Within minutes it was obvious to Barb and Mary that their mother was probably suffering a stroke and needed medical intervention fast. Fran's words began to slur slightly, blood pressure was rising. 911 was called. The ambulance rushed her to the emergency room at Jordan Hospital.

Members of the Doyle family gathered, filling the waiting area, pouring out into the hospital lobby and beyond. Each one offered Art words of comfort, but without tangible information on his wife's condition, nothing really reached him. As bits and pieces began to filter out from the emergency unit things did not look good. Finally, maybe in part to clear out this large, somewhat unruly group gathered, the emergency room nurse announced that Fran would be admitted and sent upstairs as soon as a room became free. There would be no visits that night.

Interminable days stretched into a week of tests, consultations and further tests. Nothing in the reports offered hope for a quick or a complete recovery. The doctor called Art to set up an appointment in his office with Art and some of his daughters. Methodically, the doctor laid out the reality of Fran's condition, concluding with the strong recommendation that Art place Fran into Beverly Nursing Home located near the Jordan Hospital. So it was. Fran was transferred the following morning.

It was one exit, about 6 miles from Barb and Dick's home. It may as well have been on Mars as far as Art's heart was concerned. Fran was not at home with him.

He grew quiet and pensive those first days, searching for strength to deal with what was happening. He pondered what he might be able to do to help Fran recover. He questioned himself about how could he be sure she ate, did the therapy, and got better? He prayed for wisdom. Finally he decided that his best recourse was to be present at her side each and every day. With this plan in mind, he set himself on a schedule. He got up early, ate breakfast, packed lunch and some goodies with which to tempt Fran if the nursing home fare did not.

Once he arrived at Beverly Manor he sat by her side in the main room. He appeared there every morning and stayed there the whole day long. He was there so much that both residents and visitors came to believe that he worked there in some capacity, so they related to him as such. A few asked him to keep an eye on their loved ones; others engaged him in conversation when their own family member was unable to respond to them. Arriving home wearily each evening, he watched a bit of television, read the *Boston Globe,* and prayed for Fran's recovery before falling into a deep, sometimes restless sleep.

Month after month saw no significant change. In fact, some days Fran didn't dress or even get up out of bed. She became confused about where she was and who was with her. On bad days she might not recognize her own children when they visited, nor realize that this man at her side each day was her husband. One day she stared blankly at him, stating that he seemed a very nice man, but what was he doing in her bedroom? Art quickly replied, "Fran, I hate to tell you, but I'm your husband and you are stuck with me." Something of the quick witted, crisp response sparked a glint of recognition, at least momentarily. Other days she was well aware of who was there, where she was and then she might insist on being taken home at once, wherever home was for her at that stage.

In the beginning, having her come home to Barb and Dick's house for a meal or going out for a drive were good distractions and enjoyable experiences. With the passage of time, she was less able to do even these simple things.

It was becoming painfully clear that Art's efforts, every single day, were not bringing back the mind, body, or spirit she once had. Fran's condition was deteriorating. In a very real sense she was slipping from him piece by piece. At some deep inner level he knew this.

As Fran completed her second year at Beverly Manor, there were signs which the nurses of the family saw as letting them know the end was nearing. More than once the family clustered together around her bed when every medical indication said that her death was imminent. Yet, each of those initial times, Fran eventually opened her bright blue eyes, smiled and rallied once more, possibly asking if someone might get her a hot cup of tea and some pie. After each scare, her children went back to their families, their everyday lives and their visiting schedules. Art continued at her side with persistent hope.

One day as they sat together in the day room watching the morning news there was a report regarding a new law that seemed ready to pass both the House and the Senate. It was aimed at finding a solution to the growing problem of the shortage of nurses. It caught Art's attention, so he listened to each detail with great interest. It would, among other provisions, fund qualified nurse's aides to study to become RNs under certain specified conditions. All this intrigued Art so he grabbed a pen and paper, quickly copying down the Washington contact number from the screen. Within days he had made his initial call to find out how this plan would be fanned out to the individual states. Art experienced the nursing shortage every day at the Manor. He saw the kindness of the aides who working diligently to care for the patients, in particular, his wife. He figured this bill might help some of them get the chance at a nursing license with the additional earning power that would bring to them and their families.

His research finally uncovered a place in Massachusetts for local applications. That was all he needed. He gathered all the info, made an appointment with the administrator of the nursing home, explained his research and a simple plan for disseminating the information and the forms to the aides. He told her how several of the aides had shared their stories with him, so he knew it was lack of money, not lack of smarts, will or energy that kept them back from their dreams. Since the administrator didn't need to do anything but ok this, she was happy to say "yes." The information and the needed application forms were given out with the next pay check. Satisfied that he had done what he could, Art settled back into regular life at Beverly Manor wondering, but never asking, if anyone had taken advantage of the available funds.

Fully three years later, a young Haitian woman, named Felipe, arrived at the front door of the mobile home on Mohawk Road where Art lived with Barbara and Dick. She was searching for a Mr. Doyle. Once she was invited inside she recognized him immediately and vice-versa. She pulled a chair over, sat right down by his side and poured out her whole story, Felipe spoke of her adoption as a child, her new parents and on and on right up to the present moment. Proudly she showed him her nursing diploma and wrapped her arms around him in a grateful hug. Felipe had read the information, sent in the forms, got the financial aid and finished her nursing studies. Her final step, the Nursing Boards, was coming up the following month. "Please," she asked, "please pray me through them." Felipe had always dreamed of becoming a nurse, but had little hope of earning enough money to support herself through school. Now she sat there before him, a proud, fully graduated registered nurse.

It was a full three to four months later when she visited again, having successfully passed her Boards. Over the next few years, Felipe returned several times. Once she was accompanied by a young man whom she introduced as her serious boyfriend. A few days after that particular visit, she called to ask Art what he thought about her male companion. She was beginning to experience thoughts and feelings leading her to believe that this might be her "prince charming." She wanted to talk it over with Mr. Doyle, to get his impressions. She believed that she could trust his wisdom.

From Joy to Heartache

On August 11, 2003 Art would be ninety years of age. His kids decided to celebrate this birthday in style. Fran thought it was a fabulous idea, adding suggestions on how it might go. Invitations were sent, plans finalized and, in late June, on a picture perfect summer day, family, friends and neighbors gathered at the community hall of Plymouth Mobile Estates. Fran was having an exceptionally good day which added immeasurable pleasure to the whole occasion. She and Art "held court" all day long. Linda Armstrong captured the whole celebration on video, later gifting them with a copy.

Art prepared a few words, a mix of memories and thanks, which he shared from his heart. Once that was delivered, he quietly sat back in his chair, basking in the joy of being surrounded by people whom he dearly loved. Both his remaining siblings were there. His sister, Helen, and her daughter, Kitty, flew in from Hawaii. His youngest brother, Paul, came up from Virginia with his wife, Mary. Fullness, a sense of well being and happiness was in the air.

The rest of the year proved to be a much harder journey. Fran began slipping noticeably within the fall months. The big difference being that she was not bouncing back. By Thanksgiving, although she went to dinner at Barb's house, she ate little, mostly slept in a big comfortable chair, seemingly not even conscious that she was there. Having experienced that disappointment in late November, no one was looking forward to Christmas day.

From the moment the aide helped Fran slip into the front seat of the car on Christmas morning, she was alert, precocious, funny and very loving especially toward Art who was not feeling up to par that day. She was dressed in a white sweater edged with delicate Christmas designs and colors. About an hour after feasting on a scrumptious dinner, Art decided to lie down for awhile. Without skipping a beat, Fran announced that she would join him. Barb tiptoed into the bedroom about fifteen minutes later, extra afghan in hand; to be sure they were warm enough. There they were fast asleep, wrapped in each other's arms. More than an hour later when they awoke, Art felt a bit better and Fran had renewed energy and purpose. She was like a woman with a mission.

Together they phoned each of their children with whom they had not yet spoken that day. Fran then enjoyed a slice of warm pumpkin pie with a double shot of whipped cream, accompanied by her beloved cup of tea. Soon after, she began to show the first signs all day of fading. It became clear that she was ready, maybe even needed to head back to the nursing home. Art hugged her, held her close for an extra moment, before helping her into her coat. It had been a blessed Christmas, a precious afternoon.

As December eased into the icy cold days of early January, 2004, Art's symptoms were not yielding to medication. The dry cough persisted, moving down into his chest, developing into pneumonia. He looked weary, anxious and depressed.

For the first week of the year, he stayed away from the Manor. Then, just when he felt he could resume his visits, Beverly Manor, noting the spread of the flu among their residents, posted and strictly enforced a No Visitors policy. This restriction jolted him further. As the second week began, Art became agitated, pacing the floor, wringing his hands. He felt his world crashing down around him. He knew he was approaching the edge of a slippery slope. The physical and emotional strain of the past two years had caught up with him.

January 13th he hit crisis point. Barb was out at that time, so he picked up the phone and called Debbie. He clearly knew that he was in bad shape. He sensed that his end was nearing. His anxiety, fears and doubts poured out. He pleaded for help...now.

Multiple calls were made. His personal physician could offer only a referral that was weeks away, nothing immediate. After rapid Internet research and a few well placed calls Deb discovered that there was a hospital on the South Shore, in Pembroke, where they had a Mental Health section. A psychiatrist there said that he was willing to see Art that very afternoon.

By the time Deb hung up from that last call and dialed the Plymouth number, Barb was home again and answered the phone. Having lived with him through the ups and downs of these past years, months and the last weeks, she was fully in accord with the proposed arrangements.

In short order, Art dressed and he and Barb drove straight up to the hospital parking lot to meet Debbie. True to his word, the psychiatrist was available for them. Things just kept moving forward from there. The interview quickly demonstrated that Art was truly coming apart at the seams. Within a matter of hours the interview was over, the decision for admittance made and processed. Art entered the hospital directly.

With Fran growing weaker each day and Art hospitalized, January was a long, heart-wrenching month for everyone. Art knew that he was receiving the care that he needed and that he was slowly recuperating. The big drawback to the setup was that being at Pembroke Hospital definitely meant that he could not visit Fran every day. The separation was terribly hard. He began to sense clearly from his daily visitors, what his own heart was telling him. Fran's days were numbered.

When Art finally received the news that she had been placed in Hospice care, he knew, no matter what, he had to be with her, even if it were only for one last time. There was complete agreement with him from every corner. His daughters worked with the staff at both places to make it happen.

Fran was dressed and ready for Art's arrival, when she suddenly became sick to her stomach. Art was already on his way. In a matter of minutes she was cleaned up, completely changed into a new outfit and once again lay resting against her pillow. Although she was pale, she looked lovely in a favorite red blouse with a delicate string of white pearls at her neck. Her nails were freshly done, their ring on her hand. She looked so peaceful propped up just a bit on her bed, as Art entered her room.

For safety reasons over the past months, her bed was kept almost at floor level with exercise type mats covering the floor on both side of the bed. With some difficulty, Art went down on his knees on the blue mat beside her, placed one hand under her head and lifting her upper body into his arms, held her firmly but gently. She eased into his embrace, her smile telling him of her recognition. Her eyes followed his every word and gesture. Fran even tried to mouth words of her own.

As he held her, Art knew that this was their final earthly good-bye. His lifelong friend and partner was leaving him. He once told Joanie, "My greatest joy is to wake up each morning, knowing I have another day to spend with your mother." He knew there were few mornings left.

As she slipped back into sleep, he placed her carefully onto the pillow, straightened a bit, staying quietly by her bedside. His lips moved but his eyes never left her face. After leaning forward and kissing her once more, he tenderly brushed her cheek. Then, slowly, needing some assistance, he rose, looking back at Fran one last time before leaving her room. Shakily he walked through the familiar corridors of Beverly Manor one last time.

The morning after his visit, Art woke early with a desire to write Fran a note. A few days later, as she lay dying, one of her daughters read his love note to her, never sure if Fran heard or understood Art's final words. About 7:00 pm. on Friday evening, January 23, 2004, Mrs. Arthur T. Doyle, his beloved wife, Fran, surrounded by her girls, breathed her last.

After receiving supportive hugs, Nancy and Joanie left the others at the Manor to drive up to the hospital in Pembroke. Someone called ahead to alert the staff of their imminent arrival. The night staff graciously set aside an empty room where the three of them could gather. Art knew before one word was spoken. He simply knew.

Three days later, in a church packed with their loved ones, the funeral Mass was celebrated. Fran's sons-in law, as pall bearers, escorted her casket up the steps, leading her into the middle aisle near the back benches. Her husband and daughters clothed the coffin in the white garment, resting two red roses, bound together with white ribbon, in the center. Art, Jr. was in the choir loft, preparing to sing the *Ave Maria.* His daughter, Lori, by his side.

Near the close of the liturgy, as Joanie was finishing the eulogy, she picked up a half sheet of paper, paused and swallowed back tears. She needed to gather herself for this last piece. Glancing in her father's direction, she began to slowly read the note that Art had written to his wife.

Dear Fran,

Thanks, once again, for sharing your life with me for the past 68 years.

We really loved each other when we got married and that love for each other only increased over these years.

I'm sure that you're now in heaven.
God willing, I hope to join you soon.
I can't wait to hold you in my arms again.

All my love,
Art

Joanie descended from the altar, momentarily laying her hand on the coffin as she passed. When she reached the first bench, Art simply open his arms and wrapped them around her. There was not a dry eye in the church. His love, their mutual lifelong love, was palpable.

Art looked thin, even fragile, as he followed the coffin down the aisle and into the rear of St. Francis Church in South Braintree. He was gently but firmly held on both sides by two of his daughters.

Family, friends, neighbors gathered round both at the burial service at Blue Hill Cemetery and later at the reception held at the VFW Hall right across from church. He drew strength from their presence, remaining among them at the Hall for several hours, listening and sharing many wonderful memories about life with Fran.

As the first shades of evening began to close in, folks began, little by little to gather their things together for travel. They offered Art their last bracing hugs and words of consolation. Then it was time for Art also to pack up and return to Pembroke Hospital.

The staff and even some of the younger patients who had begun to look to and relate with Art as a kindly grandfather figure, could not have been gentler or more considerate of him. They received him back the evening of the funeral as if he were extended family, promising to care well for him. One of the male staff members, in particular, who had a reputation for being a tough, no nonsense guy, was especially good to Art, doing all he could to ease the pain of this loss.

It was not time yet for Art to return home.

Life Without Fran

Art was totally convinced that he would follow Fran shortly, definitely before the year ran its course. He spoke of it often, with ease and a deep peace. This was simply how it would be and he was fine with that. In fact, that is what he longed for. But... after sleeping and waking, sleeping and then waking again and again each day for several months, he got an inkling that this mystery of his own life and death was beyond his power to comprehend much less, in any way to command.

In spite of much time spent talking this over with his Maker, nothing either consoling or enlightening surfaced, yet he continued to ponder. One afternoon he came across a poem imaging the events of one's life as parts of a puzzle. Only when that last piece was put into place would you see the whole picture. This moved him into the mode of putting his earthly affairs in order. With each piece completed, such as selling the family home on Hollingsworth Avenue, he hoped against hope.

Art held strongly to his faith, spending hours in his bedroom "hermitage." He attended daily Mass on television, prayed the rosary, read or perhaps selected one of the programs on the Catholic channel. Once, after a half hour of listening to Mother Angelica, he changed channels commenting, "I really think that she could use some updating." He had discriminating tastes.

At times, as he intended to choose x channel, his finger would unintentionally strike some other button and send the whole system into utter chaos. With great chagrin, he glared at the snow filled screen until either Barb or Dick saved the day with a corrective re-clicking of the right buttons. He never did lose this sleight of hand skill for sending almost any television program into a most annoying winter wonderland.

Slowly Art began to accept that for now, he simply had to wait in this darkness of uncertainty about his future. During his time at Pembroke hospital he had learned some good coping skills and was trying to put them into practice. He also picked up a love for hot cereal plus a few new phrases that caught everyone's attention as they slipped into conversations now and again like, " Tell her to get over it!" or "Suck it up and move on. Life's not always fair."

There was another kind of darkness that was gradually invading his life. He needed an ophthalmologist because he was having difficulty reading or watching television. Things were just not as clear as before. Lights seemed glaring. Reading, even with his regular glasses on, was wearying. An appointment was set.

After examining him, the eye doctor declared that Art had cataracts in both eyes. Without skipping even a beat, without asking questions about his healthy or agility, the doctor rolled right on, stating that considering that Art was approaching ninety years of age, he, as a doctor, would not suggest surgery. His words were like a death sentence to Art. His face immediately registered the confusion and pain. The impact of the doctor's unequivocal statement was not lost on Nancy, who was right there accompanying her father. The crestfallen look on Art's face cut her to the core. Steadying her voice, she asked the nurse to take Art out into the waiting room.

She then lit into the doctor, telling him in no uncertain terms that he did not know her father. Who was he to refuse to let this healthy man have a relatively safe surgery that would give him back one of the daily enjoyments of his life? As her rising voice penetrated the silence of the waiting room, Art could feel a sense of utter relief wash over him. He knew, without a doubt, that eventually he was going to have this surgery with another doctor. He was going to see well again. Art gave his daughter a grateful hug before she helped him into his coat and out into the elevator.

Thanksgiving came and went. The first Christmas was approaching but he had little enthusiasm for the season. The day after the Thanksgiving celebration he almost dutifully pulled out the Christmas card list. Scanning the list he felt completely overwhelmed at the prospect of writing even one card. Art and Fran always did the cards together, meticulously checking off each person on their well-kept list to be sure no one was skipped. It was a post-Thanksgiving ritual that they enjoyed. They sent them out early, then sat back and enjoyed the incoming cards, letters and especially each year's updated family photos. Often theirs was the first

Christmas greeting that many people received for the season. Part of Art wanted to keep in touch, but after putting them away and taking them out two days in a row he knew that he simply had no energy around it, maybe next year.

Barbie and Joanie were sitting around the dining room table as he related these feelings to them. Later they talked about what they might do, eventually coming up with a creative plan. They would get Carol in on it too. If he could tell them what he wanted to say in a letter, they would buy Christmas paper, type it, make copies, and mail them off to everyone in his address book. When Art heard the suggestion, he lit up. He loved the idea and immediately set about scribbling a few notes on paper. He promptly handed it over to them, telling them to add or subtract. His scribes and secretaries did add a few more newsy lines to the letter, bought stamps and began the mailing process.

The letters went out far and wide. Art did not have to wait long for results. He perked up as he received the in-coming mail from even more family and friends than usual. He laughed to himself as he got compliments on his letter. There were even hopes expressed that he would keep up this new family tradition. This idea was a keeper.

Even as Art was moving unsteadily within this difficult phase of his life's journey, there were very different movements afoot within the broader Doyle family and the world outside.

In the ordinary cycles of large families, when there is death, often soon after, there is new life. And so it was. Owen

Connor and John Jepson were four and three when Fran died. Within months after her death her grand-daughters, Elicia, then Jean, and her grandson Michael's wife, Heidi, became pregnant. The older boys were eventually joined by three more handsome male siblings or cousins: Connor Jepson, Mason Connor, and James (Jimmy) Tubridy. When the next newborns were announced there was special rejoicing because three adorable little girls were soon to join the growing family: Katherine (Kate) Jepson, Chloe Connor and Amy Huerta Cavanaugh (Shevonne's daughter). Each new baby who cradled in Art's strong arms seemed to gift him with an additional spark of life. He was a family man to the core, one who loved kids. Each one was special to him. He had an innate sense of how to convey that feeling of specialness so that each child somehow felt that he or she was, without a single doubt, Grandpa's favorite.

There was an empty space in Art's heart, one that no one would ever fill. Every once in a while you could catch something of this in his eyes, in that far away expression, that shadow of sadness crossing his face. Yet, there was no denying that he came alive watching his children reach the stage where they were now welcoming grandchildren. A few of his grandchildren were having children and proudly bringing them for that first photo op with Grampy or Great-Grandpa. One set even named him Big-Gramps. At this stage, what they called him didn't matter to him at all.

As the younger ones visited him, they often took over his somewhat calm, ordered lifestyle. They climbed up into his comfortable electric chair, gleefully pressing buttons that sent him way back or forward, sometimes at dizzying speeds that sent the grandmother flying across the room to save him, easing Art back to earth and hiding the remote control fast.

Some little ones took baby steps hanging onto his newly acquired walker. Jimmy eventually reached the stage where he wanted to know why Grampy could not walk any faster, for Jimmy could now outrun him with ease. When they ate lunch with him, they were happy imitators squirting whipped cream six inches high on their pudding or ice cream. When Barb began babysitting her grandson, Jimmy, Art felt a responsibility to re-sharpen his child caring skills, feeding techniques, entertaining and putting down to nap abilities. Sorry, there was one firm exception, his diapering days were over.

Another thing that energized Art was the fact that the hometown teams: the Red Sox, the Patriots, Celtics and even the Bruins were having some exceptionally good years. He was especially thrilled with the Red Sox. He had waited 86 years to see them not only beat those blessed Yankees in a real upset, but also go the whole nine yards to win the World Series in a real upset. They did it with style in a spectacular finish to the 2004 baseball season. He needed a minor procedure done on the day that he figured would be the final game of the series. He was booked for an early morning appointment. Art begged the doctor to give him the smallest possible dose of anesthesia. He was not going to sleep through what he instinctively felt was going to be a glorious

Red Sox moment. He never missed one single pitch of that winning game. A repeat performance in 2007 was simply icing on the baseball cake.

Art and Dick watched the Patriots' games together each weekend. They thrilled as the victories mounted up and the team had another division championship under its belt. Their delighted roars filled the house when the Patriot's big victory came in the Super Bowl of 2004. Then they 'cried' together when, after a fabulous 16-0 season the Patriots lost to the New York Giants in the big one. Art relished every aspect of the throws, maneuvers and strategic plays of the team. He got especially engrossed in following the ongoing growth in skills of their quarterback, Tom Brady.

With a new powerful set of key players and great team cohesion, the Celtics finally showed their stuff going all the way to the clincher in the 2008 playoffs, defeating the power-filled Lakers and capturing the NBA title. Art relished it all.

Art watched a daily dose of local and national news. If anything special was afoot, CNN and the Situation Room were added. Every once in a while his intake of news had to be curtailed, like when the earthquake disaster hit Haiti. Art was sure he heard that the earthquake struck Hawaii and he panicked, needing to know if his sister Helen and her family were okay. Literally, Debbie had to call Helen and have her talk to her brother, in person, before he could calm down and know that she was okay. That was more than enough news for one day.

At noon Art sharpened his wits watching "Who wants to be a Millionaire," and then later it was "Jeopardy." He devoured the *Boston Globe* which Dick had delivered to him in Plymouth and later George continued the tradition daily, faithfully placing it on Art's meal tray each evening.

He was a challenging checkers player, winning outright or if not, chiding you into the best of three, usually taking the final victory. He tried teaching each young one how to play, even if they were not totally interested. In the initial stage certain concessions were made to age or skills, but little by little the rules were slipped in. If you actually won, you earned it. John Jepson was one of the last of the great-grandchildren to keep at the checker lessons. At first Art let John win a game here or there by relaxing a few rules. Then one day he decided John was ready for the big times and applied all of them. After one such game John told Carol, his grandmother, that he now knew for sure that Grampa was getting forgetful because, "He forgot how we used to play checkers before and came in with a bunch of new ideas." John had just lost two games!

Some of the older kids who had recently gotten their drivers' licenses might drop by to check up on Grampy, while showing off what might be their secondhand wheels, but definitely was their new found freedom. They usually ate with him, chatted a bit, and then hit the road again. Sometimes, after a day of visits Art might withdraw into himself, remembering how he and Fran would spend hours together after a family gathering, sharing how they saw this child's or grandchild's personality or life unfolding; what dreams or concerns they had for them; what they might do to encourage or support. There simply was no substitute for the intimacy of those ordinary moments they used to share.

In January of 2007, another whole generation came into being when a daughter, Paige Doyle, was born to Lindsay Doyle, who was the daughter of Danny Doyle, son of Arthur Doyle Jr, son of Arthur Doyle, Sr. That meant a fifth generation of the Doyle clan had begun. Within the first months, Lindsay brought Paige south from Maine to meet her great, great grandfather. Her birth, in particular, gave Art a special kind of pleasure. He seemed to relish the role of being the patriarch of this expanding family, which later included Paige's younger brother, Seth. Art proudly tucked a photo of the five generations into the envelope with the next Christmas letter.

At times Art had energy to delve into small projects, the trappings of which seemed to expand like rising dough, filling much of the physical space in the Plymouth mobile household. Quietly, but progressively, he stretched his domain from the back room, down the hall into a small office space, then slowly but surely overflowing onto the dining room table. He claimed it all, plus his electric chair in the living room with his meal tray right beside it.

The years were starting to creep up on Art. Although he passed his driver's test again, to everyone's dismay, and renewed his license as late as 2003, his hearing was going, making him something of a hazard on the road. Returning from Braintree to Plymouth late one afternoon around sunset, he entered a construction area with unfamiliar driving patterns, became confused and ended up scraping the side of a small pickup truck. Realizing this, he pulled over to the side of the road. Two burly looking men from the truck approached his car yelling, shaking their fists, and actually threatening him. He was shaken as he watched them approaching his door, not sure how he could defend himself.

Thankfully, within minutes, a policeman from the construction site appeared on the scene and told the men, in no uncertain terms, to back off. Once insurance information and essential documents were exchanged, the officer gave Art the okay to pull his car out and leave the scene; detaining the occupants of the pickup truck long enough to be sure they did not follow him. All the way home Art's heart pounded. He was relieved to pull safely into the driveway on Mohawk Drive and turn off the motor. His hands shook slightly as he removed the keys from the ignition. He rested his head against the back of the seat for a few moments trying to compose himself before he got out and climbed the few steps to the house.

After that incident, Art drastically cut back on driving excursions except for the local roads. He drove himself down to the waterfront, shopping, or other minor trips. That was the extent of it. Finally one day, basically without incident or lengthy explanations, he simply put the car keys on the living room table and never really drove outside the compound again. In spite of this degree of surrender, for years, whenever he spoke of the red car, it was his car he was talking about, no matter who drove it.

Gradually, he also accepted his need for support while getting around, moving from a cane to a walker, with final concessions to a wheelchair, but only for shopping expeditions or longer trips.

One such excursion was to Foxwoods Casino in Connecticut. The year of his 90th birthday he received some play money, so he invited anyone who wanted to, to celebrate with him at the Casino. Four of his daughters were able to join him. His luck was a mixed bag, but he relished an excellent meal at the buffet, and even allowed a waitress to loudly sing a chorus of "Happy Birthday" amidst applause from the tables around. Thus began a birthday tradition that lasted five years.

No one ever came away rich, but each year Art looked forward to the celebration and accompanying trip to Foxwoods and savored the memories for weeks after. When he didn't win, usually one or more of his daughters did. Deb and Nancy seemed to have the best luck, but everyone had a blast. When Art had spent his energy and money, he would once again stretch out in the back of the red station wagon, which was lavishly cushioned by comforters and pillows, and slept like a baby all the way home. His pockets may not have been jingling with cash, but as Carol noted in her eulogy, "He was the richest man I knew, in all the ways that count."

At one period, Art became weaker than normal, was assessed by health care personnel and placed in hospice care. At first the family was quite concerned sensing that it signaled that his end was near. Yet, as time went on he seemed to arrive at some plateau and did not get any worse. During that period, Art made a clear decision to handwrite a Do Not Resuscitate note, a medical DNR declaration. He signed it, made copies on his Xerox machine and gave one to each of his children, put one in his wallet, taped one to the middle of the glass door of the china closet in the living room and had his wishes put on record with his doctor and the hospice caretakers. He was in no doubts about this one and wanted to be sure that no one else was either. If his moment came, he wanted no one to interfere with his final journey.

The hospice workers were wonderful with him, so they were almost sad, a year later when the head nurse, after a thorough physical examination, declined to have him continue in their care. His stabilizing condition simply did not warrant their services any longer. In a word he graduated from Hospice, as it said on the form, "... for failure to die."

During that hospice year, two special people, Edie and John, entered his life as his respite care volunteers. Edie was a married woman who had a husband and three sons about college age. She came each week to be with Art, giving Barb and Dick much appreciated time for other things. Over time, a deep and wonderful relationship grew between Art and Edie. They were good with one another, shared on many levels; watched TV together, had lunch, and taught each other different games. Edie was faithful to him. His trust in her grew strong so that sometimes Art told her things about the family that he had not shared with others. He looked forward to her visits, and after she left, he often spoke about how he spent the time with her. Even later when he moved back to Medfield, which was roughly a forty-five minute drive away, Edie found her way there to spend time with Art right up until the end. She was like an adopted daughter and a friend all rolled up into one.

John was most interesting to Art for very different reasons. He had been a priest who served in the parish where Art had lived in South Braintree. John had left the priesthood, married, and now had a grown daughter. John and Art had long, searching conversations together about the Church, faith, sports, and life in general. John gave Art his own Bible, which Art proceeded to read in conjunction with the daily readings used during the Mass he attended each morning. Eventually, John's wife was diagnosed with cancer and John needed to take her to appointments and be a closer support to her during this rough time. Art and John never entirely lost touch. John showed up now and again to stay connected.

As Art reread and began clearing away his Christmas cards, he looked up at the newly-hung calendar, shaking his head in utter disbelief. It was now the year 2009. It amazed him to realize that he would be 96 years old in the summer and, as he put it, "I am still hanging around here." Once in a while he commented to a visitor that he so wanted to give Barb and Dick back the privacy of their own home and the freedom they used to enjoy. For now, that was not possible.

Then one spring like afternoon in May, Barbie suddenly began to feel rather sick. At first it seemed like it might just be stomach cramps, but then came a wave of abdominal pains that increased in severity as the hours labored along. Barb decided that she would try to sleep it off, willing it to be gone by morning. By 2:00 a.m. she still lay awake struggling in the dark, until she knew she could not stand it any longer. She shook Dick awake, alerting him to her situation. She had to go to emergency. He searched for the light switch, grabbed his cell phone and called Nancy, waking her from a sound sleep. In a semi-fog she dressed, grabbed her keys and in a few minutes was behind the wheel headed south from Kingston to be with Art, while Dick helped Barb into the car and sped off to the Jordan Hospital. After hours of tests, the diagnosis was clear. It was a gall bladder attack and surgery was immediately set for later that morning. Once Barb was admitted, Dick headed home to catch some shuteye so he could be up and at the hospital in time for the operation. He needed to be at the hospital with Barb. Art needed to have someone at home with him. He could no longer be alone in the house for any length of time.

Once it was light, the phone calls began. News spread quickly about Barb's condition and her up-coming surgery. Everyone kicked into high gear. Carol, Nancy, Jean, Elicia, Jodi responded as they could. Coverage was set up for the next day or so, until a more permanent arrangement could be worked out. When all the conversations were finished and options considered, Art was heading back to Medfield, to re-enter the Soligan household. It was, of necessity, a somewhat abrupt, quick move without enough time to process everything with Art piece by piece.

Given his age, this rather sudden packing, shifting of place and changing of ordinary circumstances naturally had consequences. His quiet, regulated world was in upheaval. Familiar sights, sounds, people and routines that formed a comfort zone around him disappeared. Although his daughters had been as caring as possible as they packed Deb's red Toyota with an initial set of his belongings; and although they had explained how Barbie would need weeks of recovery after her surgery, Art just could not or would not process it all. He was confused, fearful and somewhat agitated as he sank into the front seat of the car heading out to Medfield.

Thankfully, there was a Red Sox game on the radio as they travelled and the Red Sox were cooperative enough to be winning the game.

Ups And Downs

Deb drove all the way into the rear of the garage so that Art could use the ramp to enter the house, which had been carefully, albeit rapidly, prepared for his arrival. Bob, the big, friendly family dog, barked his best welcome and would have knocked Art over completely as he leapt forward with excitement, had Fred not held his leash tightly. Unbeknownst to anyone at first, there quickly developed an unspoken relationship between Bob and Art which resulted in the dog's gaining almost thirty pounds their first year of life together.

Art viewed his surroundings carefully. Not much seemed familiar to him after almost eight years of living in Plymouth. Not remembering how things looked proved a minor problem. There was something more basic gnawing at him from day one. It took a few weeks for him to put his anxiety into words. With one person here or another there he began asking "Do I have a place where I really belong?" "Am I going to move back again to Plymouth once Barbie gets better, or will I be staying where I am permanently?" "Is it okay for me to stay here?" Questions like these affected his sleep, his appetite and his relationships. He couldn't settle in.

Late on a cloudy Sunday morning, Debbie and George relaxed at the kitchen table talking with Joanie who was up for one of her monthly weekends. Puzzled by Art's behavior, they were sharing different experiences or conversations each had had with him. The longer they spoke the clearer it became what was at the core of Art's unrest. With this realization, they left the kitchen, heading down the corridor to his room, Bob in tow. George edged close to Art's bedside before he spoke. Art, who had been sitting reading, looked up at his visitors. His gaze was a mix of concern and curiosity. Addressing him as Mr. Doyle, George began by clearly welcoming Art to Medfield, saying how happy he, Debbie and his kids would be if he chose to stay with them in their home and make it his own from now on. He promised Art that they would care for him lovingly as long as was needed.

Art's eyes never left George's face as he spoke to him. His whole being drank in every word. His facial muscles softened, a smile crossed his face and lit up his moistening eyes. When Art finally spoke, his words tumbled together at first, but he persevered, pouring out his relief and gratitude. You saw a difference in his physical appearance almost immediately. Although Debbie and every single one of his other daughters had said this same kind of thing to him during the whole transition time, being part of the generation that he was, Art apparently needed to hear the man of the house welcome him and expressly invite him to stay there. Once George did that, everything changed, peace returned, daily life could now find its rhythm.

For that to happen though, help needed to be found during the daytime, so that Debbie could do her ordinary household work and get some rest in the afternoon into the evening, before she began her night shift as a hospice nurse. She worked from home, but had reports, calls from worried family members, plus on-site visits as needed. These trips to a hospice patient's home could be miles away from Medfield and might involve end-of-life decisions with the emotional toll that accompanies such choices. After her return home, there were her reports to complete before her shift would end. Steady help that could consistently cover days, care for Art and offer Debbie some peace of mind in order to get sleep was sorely needed. It was not that family members didn't help. They did, but that was far from enough as Art's decline continued.

Thus, an agency was contacted and Godfrey entered the equation. Godfrey was a middle aged Ugandan with a bright smile and a strong British flavor to his accent. His speech patterns made ordinary communication with Art a bit hard and the mutual understanding of instructions and replies a real challenge. Godfrey worked specific hours during the day. It was not ideal, but it was a starting place.

Deb wrote out detailed instructions regarding Art's meals, activities he enjoyed, medications he took, morning and evening rituals, and care of his bedroom. Nothing was left to the imagination. Deb knew what was needed, how it ought to be done and knew how vital it was to have consistent messages and practices that Art could gradually accept as normal for his daily life. It would give him assurance.

Art was presented with an orange whistle that hung loosely around his neck, readily available for use when he needed help. Having been a basketball referee for years, this struck a familiar chord and he readily agreed. The shrill sound could have deafened anyone unfortunate enough to be beside him when the blowing began. There was obviously nothing wrong with Art's lungs.

This hourly work arrangement, carefully conceived and enacted, was short-lived. All too soon it became abundantly evident that assistance was really needed around the clock. On all levels it seemed that a live-in aide was probably a better solution. Changes were negotiated with the Agency and Godfrey began to live –in from Monday morning until Friday noon.

A monitor was set up in Art's room so that when no one was physically with him, it was still possible to see, hear and check on him. Art was not one bit thrilled with this new system, but knew after his first complaints that he was totally outvoted by his daughters and caretakers, so gritting his teeth, he conceded. On weekends the question, "Who has the monitor?" was a common query. It was a key part of the safety plan.

Art had developed a talent for suddenly throwing his legs over the edge of the bed and heading out, behind them, even though at this stage his balance and strength would not allow him to stand on his own. With the monitor, Art's movements were meant to always be in someone's view. At times Deb,

Godfrey or even relatives who were visiting, noticed suspicious movements and sprinted down the hall to get to his bedside before he got into full flung falling mode.

The live-in setup worked better. Things were not perfect but it was an improvement. From Friday afternoon through Sunday different members of the Doyle family took turns trying to give the coverage needed. Deb instructed each caregiver how to lift Art without hurting him or oneself; how to give Art the same clear instructions as she did; prepare meals he would actually eat; give his pills and re-set his TV again and again. He had that restless finger that wandered across the buttons of the remote messing things up on a daily, often hourly basis.

Some folks felt more confident than others being responsible for Art's care, but no one had any doubts about what they were to do. Gratefully, they also knew that Debbie was usually somewhere around the house, ready to help if needed. Deb could have issued certificates to family members for completion of basic training as home health care aides.

After a while, things overlooked in the beginning as isolated incidents, coalesced into an undeniable negative pattern. Godfrey sank into an emotional slump. As a result he was sleeping through the whistle; not doing the laundry or cleaning that were part of the agreement, talking incessantly on his cell phone, and spending more time in his room than with Art or anything else he needed to do. Deb could not sleep for fear that Godfrey would not hear or respond to the whistle. A few nights she had been awakened from a deep sleep in her room all the way downstairs by its penetrating shrill, but Godfrey, whose room was only steps away from Art's, never appeared out of his room at all. This was dangerous. It could not continue.

John and then Peter, the agency's new replacements proved to be no better. Although a side rail was put up early on, Art had a talent for scooting down to the end of his bed and landing with a thump onto the floor. Sometimes he got wedged in so uniquely between the bureau and the bed that it took an organizational genius to figure out how to get him up without further bodily damage. Miraculously there were never any fractures, but bruises and scrapes abounded. A decision was made: enough with the men! They acted more like Art's companions than responsible caretakers.

A wider search began in earnest. Fortunately, a friend of one of Debbie's friends, knew a family that worked with agencies, but who also took contracts with individual families. Thus, Rosette Nanynge arrived, interviewed, and took the position in the fall of 2009. Within days, everyone knew it was the right person. She, also came from Uganda, knew the Catholic faith, had a sunny personality, a husband and three kids. She was attractive, warm, and friendly. After a slow start, Art and Rosette hit it off well. Art, having lived with eight females around him most of his adult life, seemed somehow more at ease with a woman caretaker. Since there was a basic acceptance between them, Art and Rosette managed to work out their communication issues one day at a time. Her smile said volumes and he responded well.

Together they watched television, played games and grew fond of one another. He tried hard, but never got her name quite right, often calling her Rockette. His hearing was going and even broad hints relating her name to Rose Kennedy failed to stick for more than an hour or so. So, Rockette it was. She responded without hesitation.

During this time, Art had been losing weight, slept longer, was more unsteady on his feet, even having days when he was not weight bearing at all and required a two-person transfer. There were moments of dizziness, confusion, or slurred speech. Years before, after a PET scan, the family was advised that there were traces of cancer cells in varied parts of his body. Putting this together, Debbie began to wonder what was really going on now. Art wanted no part of hospitals, or tests. Dr. Kwan, his new primary care doctor, suggested that the local hospice group be contacted to evaluate him.

The nurse case worker came and did a thorough check. Once she received all Art's past records, including those from the hospice organization on the South Shore, she said that it was appropriate for him to be in hospice care once again. This time she would not expect him to be getting better, given his age and these present signs of decline. Art took it all in saying that he was okay with this turn of events.

As life moved on, with Art adapting to his new environment, feeling peaceful, finding a level of ease, having great care, plus a parade of visitors, he began to improve somewhat. Yet, undeniably there was a permanent, much lower threshold for what was now considered normal health for him.

None of these medical determinations interfered with Art's enjoyment of sports on the big television in the den. Debbie and George, being real sports fans themselves, had purchased a television set with a wide 55-inch screen. Art confessed that whatever he watched, he had the exhilarating feeling that he was right there almost on the playing field itself. In football season, he chuckled that he ducked once feeling like he might be tackled by the fullback. He loved every minute of it. As they watched the games year-round, but especially during the football season, George usually treated everyone to a delicious in the comfort of your living room- style tailgating party. Curled up in his big comfortable chair, usually draped with an electric blanket, no matter the season, Art was a happy camper.

In November, when the admitting hospice nurse arrived for Art's six- month evaluation, he seemed, at least during her visit, more like his old charming self. Everything she asked him health wise, received a cheery "It's just fine." With his walker, he even managed to parade around the kitchen with a more or less steady gait, throwing in a joke or two along the way. Debbie shook her head and rolled her eyes with a few of his responses. Yet, at the end of the visit, the nurse's own findings confirmed that although he was slipping in some areas, there was no evidence of immanent life threatening conditions. The nurse explained that with the new stricter state regulations that were being implemented, Art was no longer eligible for hospice care. With a broad grin, Art accepted this notice of a second hospice graduation, adding confidently, "I am not a quitter. I will be back to complete this course yet."

This was a setback for Art's caretakers. Now there would be no outside help, no nurse coming in regularly to check on him and adjust meds or procedures. The Doyle women and their kids offered as much support as they could. Jodi, Art's grand-daughter, who had recently lost her job in a family run restaurant where she had worked for years, came in to help in between job searches. She was a Godsend but still it was not steady help. Debbie, felt that two people were now needed at all times when transferring Art from one position to another. He simply no longer had the strength to cooperate as he once could. Ordinary activities of every daily living became harder and harder for him to perform. Debbie began considering her alternatives.

Days were growing shorter, darker and colder. Winter apparel appeared. Heat went on, at a temperature higher than usual to ensure that Art stayed warm. As the Christmas season rolled around, boxes were brought down from the attic and piled in the den, waiting for the branches of the huge freshly cut tree to settle naturally into place, so they could receive scores of decorations. The tree amply filled the space in the high-ceilinged family room. Art took up his electric chair vantage point to relaxingly oversee and enjoy the trimming process. The tree was a beauty even before it was carefully dressed with literally thousands of lights and hundreds of ornaments. It lit up the whole room with an air of celebration. The fresh pine smell that filled the room, the festive spirit the tree and decorations brought were delightful. The whole scene had a peaceful way of evoking warm, wonderful, if sometimes bittersweet memories of years gone by.

Christmas week passed all too quickly and Art was not thrilled at all when he realized that this lovely tree had to come down right after the holidays. There was no choice that year because on New Year's Eve Deb and her family were travelling to Virginia to attend a Soligan family wedding. The tree would simply be too dry to stay up until they returned. It had been up for two whole weeks already. So, Art took a nap instead of watching the beauty of the lights go dim before his eyes, as an all hands on deck de-decorating ritual played out after lunch one day before they left town. His indoor winter wonderland was gone.

Nancy was ringing in New Year with her Dad that year. He slept earlier in the evening, in order to be alert enough to watch the ball drop at Times Square. He and Joanie had once braved freezing temperatures to actually be there in person. By mutual agreement, it was a wonderful but never to be repeated experience. Nancy was delighted that he enjoyed this event because she had been ushering in each New Year with the Times Square descending ball for thirty-plus years.

She stepped into his room about 11:50 p.m. comforter in hand and curled up beside him on the bed. When she got herself settled and focused on the television, she realized this was not New York City by any stretch of the imagination. Art was totally engrossed in a religious service from Rome where young round-faced boys were pouring their hearts out in song. Nancy understood nothing of what they were singing and knew her Dad did not either. She wondered out loud why he was listening. He smiled, saying that something of their sincerity, of their faces and singing made him feel peaceful and happy. Obviously, he had totally forgotten about the New York festivities. Nancy paused a moment, then decided that whatever warmed her Dad's heart and gave him joy carried the night. The crystal ball that descended to shouts of thousands at Times Square went unwatched in Medfield. As the children, looking like cherubs from a medieval art work, finished the final chorus, 2010 arrived. Art and his daughter hugged one another, wishing for the best in the year to come. Shortly thereafter, Art fell into a peaceful sleep for the rest of that night.

Then Came the Spring

Finally the winter months loosened their chilly grip on Mother Nature. A refreshing fragrance filled the March morning air, and warm breezes began melting the last dreary patches of snow from the back yard of the house on Ledgetree Road. Hints of baby green shoots were visible on the trees and in the corners of the yard nearest the house. Art was pleased to notice them from the wide kitchen window during breakfast time. At the same time he was tired, feeling his age and knowing in his depths a more profound readiness to let go.

Some days, walking from the bedroom to the living room, even leaning on a walker, seemed like a full marathon. The wheelchair became his new legs. Yet, even there it was different. Earlier on he could propel himself down the short corridor to the kitchen, only needing help to navigate around the counter to get to his place at the kitchen table. Of late, he readily let anyone available push him along, guide him to the table, set up his food, and maybe assist him with eating it too.

From time to time, especially in the mornings, Art began experiencing not just sudden dizziness but actual blackouts. Generally, he was fortunate enough to be near the bed and could land safely onto its soft broad surface. Then one day, with no apparent cause, he experienced tremors, like a seizure or perhaps a TIA. It did not last long but it caused increasing concern. Art mentioned that this was somehow different. It hurt a little. One of these events happened a day that Deb and Barb were both at the house together. There were tremors, slurred speech and his eyes were without focus. Afterwards he was simply limp. They called Dr. Kwan's office, getting an appointment that very afternoon.

Art stayed in bed, sleeping for several hours before they got him up and ready for the trip to the doctor's office. When he awoke he was alert, focused and looked, not great, but better. By the time they entered Dr. Kwan's office, it was like another man appeared, one who could speak clearly, stand relatively well and had a better blood pressure reading than his caretakers. This person who also could be counted on to appear at times when the visiting nurse or a physical therapist came to the house, was nicknamed "Perky Pete". Not even a quick change artist was that good. Pete seemed to intuit when medical personnel were even remotely on the horizon and dredged up energy from some underground stream to surprise everyone. Once the event was over, he collapsed back into his normal state.

Utterly frustrated, Barb and Deb left the office feeling that they were probably seen as overreacting females who needed to chill out. If Deb and Dr. Kwan had not been communicating regularly before that day, it might have been so.

In the weeks that followed, the incidents of severe weak spells, confusion, even varieties of hallucinations, sightings of orbs occurred off and on with differing intensities. They took a real toll on Art's already weakened memory. He searched for ordinary words to finish a sentence or even begin one. Nights found him worried, obsessed, restless, up and down to the bathroom five or six times in one night. He ate less, choked on puddings or even on fluids. "Tuck your chin in," became a constant meal time chant to prevent choking.

Art was so sure Fran would come for him that year on April 30th, 2010, their seventy-fifth wedding anniversary. When the anniversary came and went he became even more disoriented, convinced that he had to find his way back to their home on Hollingsworth Avenue right away, for that was where Fran would come to find him and bring him with her at last.

Some days of May were totally "in-bed" days. Art was losing interest in TV, the newspaper, most foods, that is except for a Friendly's strawberry sundae or milk shake or maybe a Dunkin Donut jelly stick. He kept his sweet tooth active and alert to the very end. Occasionally, there were days when his stamina made a brief re-appearance. If visitors arrived, especially accompanied by kids, he might be roused. He even made it outside one warm day when Carol, Elicia and her three kids visited. Eyeing the basketball in the garage, he asked for it and shot a few baskets from his wheelchair, delightfully surprising everyone, even himself.

Such days were rare exceptions now. Generally, caretakers were getting little or no sleep, which often meant that Debbie was not either, because she was being called upon more. Everything required two people and when Art was really unsteady, a third person for safety sake. George was called into service more often. Even in this weakened condition, Art still might manage to squirm out of the bed and fall. His guardian angel worked overtime. After one such incident, requiring the Medfield Fire Department, a hospital bed was decided upon. Although it annoyed everyone by taking forever to arrive, it finally came.

From first sight of his new bed, he despised it intensely. Even though it was meant to keep him safe, the smaller bed with built-in protective sides confined his movements more than he wanted to tolerate. He tried to scale those bars with the same determination as an Everest mountain climber going for the heights. Art was not always fully aware now of what he was doing, so someone had to be near him at almost all times.

Mostly, he could be found in his room now, so when young ones came and no parents were in sight, one of them might just climb right into his cool new bed. Others might bring special drawings they had done for him at school. These were shared with elaborate explanations, and then taped on the wall near his bed so he could continue to enjoy them after they went home. He seemed to like their company

Depending on their ages and other circumstances, parents began talking with their kids of Grandpa's need to leave them and go home to God. They took it in or not as they were able. After Mason visited his great-grandfather one afternoon, he came into the kitchen looking sad. He did not like to see him so sick, nor did he want him to go away. Michael, Heidi and Deb tried to comfort him while Chloe, his sister, picking up the mood, stuck close by. They knew that Jimmy would be arriving shortly with Jean, his mom. They were a bit concerned how he would react having spent time with his great-grandfather two days a week since his birth. Both his Mom and Barb, his grandmother had been preparing him for the visit.

When they arrived, Mason, feeling better now, took Jimmy down to the room. He followed Mason right up close to the bedside. For a few moments he looked very carefully at his grandfather, concluding that he was having a sleep. He turned to Mason and declared, "He's breathing. We can go play outside."

Nights became interesting. Once in awhile Art spoke of late night visitors, ones that no one else saw. One morning he related in detail a great 60's party that he had with his old friends Eddie and Jimmy. There was lots to eat, to talk and joke about. When asked if Fran was present, he responded that she was not able to be there, but had called in and chatted. The veil between this world and beyond was growing thinner, Art's sense of who was alive or dead less certain.

Art waxed and waned in his orientation to present reality. One day he might be unsure what to do with his sandwich, another he was fine. His caretakers' abilities to cope were being challenged to the max. Some days, more so nights, were almost beyond the pale. Could it possibly be that after all the efforts throughout all these years, Art might have to, at this last juncture, go into a nursing home? The possibility was staring them in the face.

Different ones leaned in this or that direction. No one could say for sure how long this might go on. Good will abounded, but honestly, human energy did not. Tears came, anger at how things were. Helplessness and even hopelessness clashed together with good old Irish guilt. Heart wrenching calls stretched into the wee hours. Alone and together the girls struggled to know what was best, what was possible. Many indicators underscored the fact that Art's time was nearing, but it had appeared that way before. More than once, they had set deadlines for making a final decision, only to have him rebound somewhat and the timeline moved forward again.

In the end it was seen as Deb's call. Art was in her house and she with George could make the determination. Whatever it was, everyone would abide by it. Debbie had seriously considered applying for intermittent FMLA- Family medical leave before. Now she believed that she would need to actually take a full six-month period.

She typed the e-mail to her supervisor at the hospice agency, stating her concern for how this would affect others on the staff, but seeing no other way. She named the week of June

20th as the time to begin her leave. In her innermost being, she knew she just had to have a little while longer, but without the pressure of her hospice work outside the house.

She also wrote a long e-mail to Dr. Kwan, offering both the big picture and the latest updates on Art's condition. She was seeking advice professionally, yes, but also she needed wisdom from an experienced, trusted medical person.

June came, so did the heat, yet Art continued to wear his signature outfit of thermal underwear, sweatpants, a dress shirt and cardigan with his glasses and a pen in the shirt pocket. Getting him to consider letting go of his thermals was an everyday basically fruitless conversation. They, plus his chair blanket, kept him warm while those around him were slipping into shorts, sleeveless tops and began checking out the fans.

Just before Father's Day, Art woke up one morning with obvious energy and enthusiasm. He wanted to be up and out of his bed, as if he sensed this surge was a gift not to be wasted even for a minute. He was talkative, clearly understandable, and happy for visitors. He was interested in the NBA championship series, cheering for another Celtic title. (Mercifully, he slept through the last ten minutes of the seventh game, when the Celtics handed the game to the Lakers on a silver platter.)

He even had the strength, that evening, to shake the living daylights out of the hated bedrails. He asked if they had been bought at the five and dime store. The response was that if they had been purchased there, they would have been torn out of place by him weeks ago. He rattled them again in reply.

On Friday, of the second week of June, Art was really restless and agitated, pushing the limits for everyone. Doing almost anything to assist him physically was a struggle. At one point Debbie looked straight at him and said, " For the love of God, Dad, calm down. You've taken care of all of us for all these years. Now, just let us take care of you." Her words hit home. Something switched inside him. He turned toward her and responded calmly and clearly, " It was my pleasure to care for all of you."

Father's Day, 2010, coincided with the twenty-eighth wedding anniversary for George and Debbie. Art got wind of it and sent Joanie out to buy him a card and restaurant gift certificate for them. They usually went out to eat together on Saturday nights.

Fred, Jodi and Joanie were all in the house that Saturday evening. Art was in a deep sleep, so George and Deb felt safe going out to enjoy a few hours of celebration, plus do some food shopping. About an hour or so after they left, Art woke up, wanted pillows to prop himself up more. He then engaged the three caretakers in a lively conversation with plenty of good laughs. When George and Deb returned they were utterly amazed. Everyone decided this was the best moment to exchange Father's Day/anniversary cards and gifts. Art read his cards, appreciating especially the ones containing his favorite scratch tickets. He handed them over to Jodi to scratch for him, and then enjoyed watching George open some of his things. Everyone went to bed peacefully that night. Jodi and Joanie slept on a blow-up mattress near his bed and, for a change, actually got some sleep.

Sunday dawned brightly, a beautiful clear day. When Deb and Joanie approached Art's side to begin the morning's ablutions, it was obvious that there had been a radical change since the last time they had checked him about 6:00 a.m. There was no response to his name, no movement, hardly even a fluttering of his eyes. His breathing was shallow and slow. As Deb checked out his vitals, she whispered that she believed this time his final journey had actually begun.

Calls were made to family members.

For most of the day, Deb and Joanie simply sat quietly by his bedside. Now and then one of them would moisten his lips, adjust his pillow or send silent messages of love and gratitude, plus a gentle okay if it was time to go. Sometimes he squeezed the hand that was lightly touching his, other times, in truth, most of the time, nothing

The day was difficult yet somehow peaceful. An air of serenity enveloped him. Every now and then a call came. He only stirred enough to respond to one or two. When Claire phoned from California mid-afternoon, he said very little in response to her words, yet, his eyes and smile showed that he drank it all in. Then releasing the phone, he closed his eyes, slipping into a deep sleep, almost before the phone was back in its cradle.

Over the next two days his children, grandchildren, great-grandchildren and friends came in and out saying little, just being with their last farewells. Even Bob silently crept into the room. Seeming to sense the reality unfolding, he carefully positioned himself under the edge of the hospital bed, fully and simply present. Voices were low. Eyes moist, sometimes the tears overflowed. Embraces were wordless. Each one tried to console the other with the knowledge that Art would soon enter the life he had yearned for, for so many years.

By Wednesday, June 23rd, his breathing was almost imperceptible, his chest hardly rising. A gentle sense surrounded him. All bedrails were removed. Art was free. Nothing confined his body or his spirit.

Art's son, Arthur, Jr. and his daughter, Claire were to arrive that day. Claire was flying from California mid-afternoon. Nancy and Joanie went to pick her up at Logan, hoping to speed her trip to the house. Arthur, with some of his family, was on his way to the house around that same time. Earlier in the day, Barbie had called Art's sister, Helen, in Hawaii and his brother, Paul, in Virginia to help them to know that the end was near.

Arthur, his oldest son Danny, Danny's wife, Victoria, and his daughter, Alicia, arrived early afternoon, warmly greeted those gathered in the kitchen and den, then walked down the corridor into Art's room. They smiled momentarily, seeing the bright Patriots' sheets covering him in the bed.

Arthur and Danny sat in the low chairs on opposite sides of his bed, as close as they could be. Victoria drew up a chair beside her husband, while Alicia stood near her Dad. After a time Victoria left in tears, joining Carol and Debbie in the kitchen. They continued sitting around the table, mulling over photo albums, giving the others their time alone with Art.

That time was not long. Victoria had only left the room for a short while, when very peacefully and quietly, without movement or sound, Art took his last breath, slipping from this world into eternity.

The car, returning from the airport with Claire, was about a mile or so away.

A Grand Send-off

No doubt about it. Art would have loved his wake and funeral. He had pre-arranged many of the details and more or less, that was how it came to pass.

The wake began on a picture-perfect summer afternoon, not a cloud to be seen in the deep blue sky. The Friday Cape traffic offered its usual challenges to those who drove south to Braintree where the funeral home was located. Yet, people joined the traffic flow and came. They filled the main room at Cartwright's, overflowing into the corridor. There were hugs, tears, stories, and even moments of resounding laughter. It was a tribute to him, a celebration of who he was. Friends and relatives, who had not seen one another since the last family event, gathered round. Neighbors, friends of his kids, even a few of his old guard Telephone Company co-workers arrived to pay their respects, accompanied by their more agile family members who understood their need to come to say "good-bye" to an old friend.

Tucked in the back corner of the main room, during the hours of the wake, was a wide screen television set up on a table, with several chairs grouped before it. On the screen was a continuously running set of photos. The first part chronicled different moments of Art's life, from his youth forward. That was followed by pictures showing Art with each of his eight children and their families. The background music added to the significance of the story the photos told, since it was four songs, each chosen for its connection to Art and Fran's life together. *I Did It My Way* was young Art's song to his Dad the night of his retirement party. *The Skaters' Waltz* was their song ever since they first met at the ice skating rink. Many people had never seen photos of Art as a chubby faced pre-schooler; nor as a tall, thin, wavy-haired young man in his twenties. The photos went the gamut, all the way through his almost 97 years. It was a great Irish wake, missing only the food and drink.

There had been times in his later years when Art wondered and even worried about the faith life of different members of his large family. So, months before his death, he decided to offer everyone a last gift as a remembrance. It was a small pamphlet of devotional prayers that he found years ago, one that he prayed with at some point each day. Art ordered 100 copies, asking that his memorial card be clipped to its cover and that a booklet be given to each child, grandchild, great grandchild, plus other relatives or friends who might want it.

No one was quite sure, as the wake began how this gift would be received. They did not need to wait long to find out. As the first booklets were handed out, with the story behind it, they were accepted as one would receive something quite precious. Word spread through the room about "Art's prayer book." People began to come forward asking if there might be a copy for them. Before the reception meal ended the next day, there was not a single copy left. One of his friends declared aloud that if Arthur Doyle found peace and solace using these prayers each day, there must be something good there and he sure wanted one.

Close family members lingered behind after the crowd had left Cartwright's, needing some more quiet time, moments alone or in small groups, before the morrow. They removed the barrier of the kneeler, circled the casket, saying little, the silence speaking for them.

Thankfully, Saturday brought another bright sunny day, warm but not uncomfortable. As the family gathered at the funeral home or across the street within the coolness of the back of St. Francis of Assisi Church, the town of Braintree was busy outside preparing for its traditional Fourth of July parade and celebration. It was only the last Saturday of June, but having been rained out the year before, they had chosen this date for their first try. The following week would be the alternate one.

Fran's birthday was the Fourth of July. This unexpected coincidence added a special touch to the day. Since town regulations stated that funerals took precedence over parades, all the finery and fanfare could be set up before hand but no music, not one single marcher could step forth until the whole retinue of funeral cars cleared the plaza in front of the church and moved beyond the parade route boundaries.

The Mass of the Resurrection, celebrated by the Pastor, Father Kevin Sepi, was beautifully simple. Father knew Art and had a warm spot in his heart for him. The Pastor first became acquainted with him personally through letters Art wrote to the parish priest asking to continue to be considered a member of this Braintree parish, even though he now lived in Plymouth. After a year of receiving Art's weekly notes and Sunday contributions to the church, Father Sepi decided to try to visit this elderly gentleman, to assure himself that he was well taken care of and to assure Art that, without a doubt, he would be buried from St. Francis Parish Church. When they finally met in Plymouth, Art was still quite fit and alert. They enjoyed a delightful conversation sharing stories, questions and a few suggestions Art had for the church. Art served as an usher for about a decade and always had some new ideas for improvements. They continued to exchange visits and letters for years after. The fact that they had built that relationship over the years gave the homily warmth, a feel of reality. It was lovingly delivered, true to Art and who he was as a man of deep faith. Father Sepi came off the altar, down to the space before the front benches and spoke right to the family members.

As the liturgy neared its end, it was time for the Eulogy, Arthur, Jr., stepped out of his bench, approaching the microphone within the sanctuary. Carol also came forward and stood a few steps behind him in silence.

He spoke slowly, his voice strong, yet full of emotion.

"Like most of you,
I have never won a Super Bowl, like the Patriots,
never won a World Series, like the Red Sox

never won an NBA Title, like the Celtics...

but you know ...
all that was really not needed, because on July 16, 1936
I hit the lottery,
won the gold medal and
won the jackpot,
when I was born the son of Arthur T. Doyle, Sr.,
the greatest man I have ever known.

I love you, Dad."

Tears caught in her throat, his younger sister, Carol, moved toward the microphone. She set down her papers, steadied herself, raised her head slightly and began.

> *"There have been many great men in history and our Dad was one of them. Dad had a way of making everyone of his eight children, sixteen grandchildren, twenty great grand-children and two great, great grandchildren all think they were his favorite.*
>
> *Being everything to everyone would have exhausted a lesser man, but Dad made it look easy."*

Carol went on to share stories of his life, his ways, his love, even a dream he once had about how it might be when he met his Maker.

> *"Dad once told my sister, Mary, he had a dream that he went to Heaven and there he met God. God said*

> *"Welcome, Arthur, a job well done, a life well lived, in fact, a gold star.*
>
> *Dad said, "Wouldn't everyone want a gold star?"*

As Carol reached the end of her sharing, she concluded:

> *"We all know he has finally gotten his wish to be with Mom. They are walking hand in hand. No more pills, canes, walkers or wheelchairs.*
>
> *We will miss him terribly, but how can we be sad?"*

They walked to their benches, hands held tightly together. Art and Fran must have smiled at their family who seemed instinctively to move closer to each other as the sharing went on, moving apart again slightly, only to make space to embrace Art and Carol as they re-entered their benches.

As the strains of the recessional song, *Let There Be Peace on Earth*, filled the church, family members and friends began filing down its front steps, welcomed by the brightness of the day. As they did this they could hardly help but be caught by the juxtaposition of sights before their eyes.

On the one hand there was a lineup of black limos and cars with signs saying Funeral attached to their car roofs, being filled by moist eyed family members. On the other hand, by now, the town was completely decked out in all its patriotic finery. Stores were awash with red, white and blue banners, stars and flags. The townsfolk (Art and Fran lived there 40 +

years) lined the streets. Kids of all ages were tugging on balloon strings, waving flags and opening coolers for drinks or lunch. It looked like a giant reception committee had gathered before them.

In spite of their tears, they had to smile as the funeral procession began its slow journey down the parade route toward the Blue Hill Cemetery. Children along the route jostled one another for a better view of the long sleek limos. Men doffed their Red Sox baseball caps, holding them respectfully across their hearts. People saluted, waved or simply watched, probably not quite sure how to respond in the mixture of this sad yet festive moment. Art and Fran, who dressed and dragged their kids to every parade within shouting distance, must have thoroughly enjoyed this sight.

The cars threaded their way along the roads into the cemetery, turning down the first lane toward the array of chairs and a large white canopy meant to protect at least the older generation from the unforgiving noontime sun. A blessing prayer was offered by the Pastor. Friends were invited to join family members in praying an Irish Blessing to complete the service.

People quietly milled around, some talking softly, others placing flowers on the coffin or gathering them up to take away and perhaps press in a book later. Some simply stood by in silence with their thoughts, prayers, or memories.

When the service was completed, the undertaker removed four angels from the corners of the casket and carefully placed them into Debbie's open hands. There had also been four angels on the corners of Fran's casket, six years ago. At that time, the angels were given to Arthur, Barbie, Mary and Claire. The remaining four sisters, Joanie, Nancy, Carol and Debbie, knowing this would happen today, were drawn into a close circle to receive, in a real sense from their Dad, an angel, a guardian to watch over each one of them in the years ahead.

Art had done some research during the year before Fran died. He had chosen and put into place for the time of their deaths and burials some small but very special touches for their children. Along the side of their tombstone he had the monument company carve the names of his eight children, so that, as they had been together throughout life, now, at least in one way, they would still be together beyond death.

Eventually people moved toward their cars, looked over the directions to the nearby reception hall and slowly began heading out. Art had planned his reception, for the Knights of Columbus Hall which is located directly across the street from St. Francis Church. The Fourth of July parade made that an impossible choice, so, chuckling at the remaining local choice, the reception was at the Sons of Italy Hall up the road a piece.

The buffet was excellent, especially because, in honor of both Fran and Art and their unremitting love for sweets, there were ever-replenished plates sporting about a dozen different desserts from which to choose. The sweet tooth trait must be family-based, since not even one crumb of dessert remained for clean-up.

The hall was full, noisy, and alive. People hung around for hours, table hopping, catching up on news. They savored every moment of being together. Only the delivery of floral arrangements and the quiet start of preparations for a 4:00 pm wedding reception being held in the same hall that day, managed to coax some reluctant folks to depart.

Woven through the conversations that afternoon was the consensus that, yes, we would all want Art back in a heartbeat, but not as he was physically and definitely not separated from Fran. We needed to let him go, to rejoice with him in his new found freedom and his longed for reunion with her.

Grief would surely have its way with each of us. It would flow through us in its own time and fashion, surprising our hearts, overtaking us in unexpected moments, in private or even public places.

No one could ever say that Art had not prepared us for his death. We knew well that it was coming. Yet, at our deepest human level, the heart space of our being, who is ever, ever ready for the finality of that last good-bye?

Irish Blessing

May the road rise to meet you,
May the wind be always at your back,
May the sun shine warm upon your face,
And the rains fall soft upon your fields.
And until we meet again
May God hold you
In the palm of His hand.

Made in the USA
Lexington, KY
27 March 2013